# 50 ACTIVE ASSEMBLIES

## *Peter Norton*

Heinemann Educational Publishers
Halley Court, Jordan Hill, Oxford OX2 8EJ
a division of Reed Educational & Professional Publishing Ltd

OXFORD  MELBOURNE  AUCKLAND
JOHANNESBURG  BLANTYRE  GABORONE
IBADAN  PORTSMOUTH (NH) USA  CHICAGO

02 01 00
10 9 8 7

**British Library Cataloguing in Publication Data**
A catalogue record for this book is available from the British Library

ISBN 0 435 30242 6

Designed by Roger Denning
Typeset by Books Unlimited (Nottm)
Printed and bound in Great Britain by Athenæum Press Ltd,
Gateshead, Tyne & Wear

**Acknowledgements**
The publishers would like to thank the following for permission to
reproduce copyright material:

Richard Aldington for the poem 'Bombardment' on p. 113; The Bible
Society/HarperCollins Publishers Ltd for the bible exracts taken from
the *Good News Bible*, UK © American Bible Society, 1966, 1971, 1976,
1992, on p. 74–5; Ted Hughes for the poem 'Six young men',
reproduced with the permission of Faber and Faber, on p. 114; The
Society of Authors on behalf of the Laurence Binyon Estate for the
poem 'For the fallen (September 1914)' by Laurence Binyon, on
p. 115; A P Watt Ltd on behalf of The Trustees of the Robert Graves
Copyright Trust for the poem 'The last post' by Robert Graves, on
p. 114; Wilfred Wilson Gibson for the poem 'A lament' on p.115.

The publishers have made every effort to trace copyright holders.
However, if any material has been incorrectly acknowledged, we
would be pleased to correct this at the earliest opportunity.

# Contents

# Introduction

**T**he preparation of interesting assemblies is a time-consuming task. In this book I have produced easy-to-use assemblies, usually involving pupils and making use of visual aids. The latter are designed further to interest the audience but require little or no additional work.

A number of these assemblies have a directly religious content while others contain values that are fundamental to Christianity, and most other faiths. Some assemblies have been written covering connected areas of the same theme. This allows you to return and develop the subject further or in a different way. Connected assemblies are listed under the 'Related assemblies' heading.

Each assembly is presented with detailed notes, enabling it to be given with a minimum of extra effort. You might wish, however, to develop or adapt the ideas further to meet your own personal teaching style.

In a number of assemblies I have suggested making use of an overhead projector and screen, to enhance the assembly's visual impact. If the equipment is not available the information could, in most cases, be produced on large sheets of paper instead.

Where I have recommended using pupils as characters in mini plays, you may wish as an alternative, to narrate yourself and direct the pupils' actions as you go along. This enables you to make use of pupils even if you do not have a form to call on for volunteers. It also cuts out the need for rehearsals.

To enhance these assemblies further you might like to start and end them with a piece of music, which could bear some relationship to the assembly theme. Suggestions might be:

| Assembly | Music |
|---|---|
| Happy New Year | 'Happy New Year' (Abba) |
| The Easter story | *The Messiah* by Handel |
| Easter traditions | 'Jesus Christ, superstar' by Andrew Lloyd-Webber and Tim Rice |
| The Christmas story | 'Saviour's day' (Cliff Richard) |

| | |
|---|---|
| Christmas cards and all that | 'I believe in Christmas' (Greg Lake) |
| Feed the world | 'Do they know it's Christmas?' (Band Aid) |
| You don't know you're born | 'Driving the last spike' (Genesis) |
| It's their world too | 'Calypso' (John Denver) |
| Robert Bruce, King of Scotland | 'The Skye Boat song' by Anne Campbell MacLeod |
| The seed sower | 'Spring' from *The Four Seasons* by Vivaldi |
| The Olympic Games | 'Chariots of fire' (Vangelis) |
| The wreck of the *Forfarshire* | Overture from *The Flying Dutchman* by Wagner |
| The boss's new clothes | 'Dedicated follower of fashion' (The Kinks) |
| Seeing is believing | 'Crocket's Theme' (Jan Hammer) |
| Probably so | 'The gambler' (Kenny Rogers) |
| The love of money is the root of all evil | 'If I were a rich man' by Jerry Bock (Topol) |
| Why 11th November? | 'It's a long way to Tipperary' by Jack Judge and Henry Williams |
| Walls have ears | 'White cliffs of Dover' (Vera Lynn) |
| The Battle of Britain | 'March of the Royal Air Force' |
| It's not a game | 'Nimrod' from *The Enigma Variations* by Elgar |
| St Valentine | 'You can't hurry love' (Phil Collins) |
| St David | 'Land of my fathers' by James James |
| St Patrick | 'When Irish eyes are smiling' |
| St George | 'Land of hope and glory' by Elgar |
| St Andrew | 'Scotland the brave' |

In the event of no obvious connection existing between an assembly and a piece of music, you might like to play either a piece of classical or contemporary music of your own choice.

# Celebrations

**E**ach of the assemblies in this section is intended to allow you to increase the pupils' awareness of a number of important celebrations and the traditions connected with some of them.

| Assembly | Theme |
| --- | --- |
| Happy New Year | *Being caring and kind throughout the year* |
| The Easter story | *Easter* |
| Easter traditions | *The origins of Easter traditions* |
| The Christmas story | *Christmas* |
| Christmas cards and all that | *British Christmas traditions* |
| Pancake Day | *Traditions behind Shrove Tuesday* |
| Chinese New Year | *Chinese New Year and the story of the twelve animals* |
| Ramadan | *The Muslim celebration of Ramadan* |
| Rama and Sita | *The story of Divali (Diwali)* |

# Happy New Year

**Theme**   Being caring and kind throughout the year

**Date**   During the first week back after Christmas holiday

**Materials**   Christmas cards with goodwill greetings

**Assembly organization**   Start the assembly by talking about New Year's Eve being seen as a time for a new start, and people making New Year's resolutions.

Ask the pupils about any resolutions they have made and ask if they have managed to keep them so far. (You might like to tell them of any resolutions you have made.)

Move on to ask the pupils what special name is given to the period of time leading up to and after Christmas. (You might want to give a clue and say it's called the ...... of goodwill.)

Next go on to talk about all the nice things that people do and say to each other during the 'season of goodwill'. Read out some of the cards you have collected with their goodwill messages. You might also talk about how, during World War I, the fighting in some areas would stop on Christmas Day and soldiers from each side would sometimes play games for the day.

Next go on to talk about how once this special day has ended or this special season is over, people usually go back to being nasty to each other and forget all the Happy New Year wishes. After Christmas Day the soldiers went back to shooting each other. Why is it we can only be nice to each other for this short period of time, called the 'season of goodwill'? Why can't we be nice all year round?

Conclude by explaining to the pupils that, although a little late, today you want them all to make with you a New Year's resolution to have:

**A year of goodwill.**

During this year of goodwill everyone at the assembly will be polite and helpful to each other and there will be no name calling and bullying. You could go on to ask the pupils to give other examples of types of behaviour that will not be acceptable, and those that will be acceptable, during this year of goodwill.

You could further emphasize this point by relating it to the Christmas message of 'Peace on Earth and Goodwill to all Men'. You could explain that this means goodwill to all people, not just at Christmas but throughout the year.

**Related assemblies** None

# The Easter story

**Theme**    Easter

**Date**    Any time in the last week of the term before Easter

**Materials**    None

**Assembly organization**    In the weeks before Easter, in advance of the assembly date, it will be necessary to rehearse the following scenes with volunteers from your form.

At the start of the assembly, get the pupils into the appropriate positions for each scene. Start by explaining that the assembly will be looking at the Easter story and some of the events leading to the crucifixion. (You may need to explain that crucifixion involved nailing men and women to a wooden cross. It was a very painful way used by the Romans to put people to death.) Jesus's last journey to Jerusalem had been made about a week before the crucifixion, on what Christians call Palm Sunday. It was so called because the people laid branches from a palm tree at the feet of the donkey Jesus was riding. (See *Matthew 21, 1–11.*)

Ordinary people liked Jesus. Because of this Jewish leaders saw him as a threat. Also, Jesus did not approve of many of the things that the people did. In his last week in Jerusalem he had thrown stall-holders and money-lenders out of the Temple. All this made him very unpopular with the Jewish leaders who wanted to get rid of him. (See *Matthew 21, 12–17.*)

Go on to explain that now you want to look at the events leading up to the crucifixion.

*Narrator*    When Jesus was in Jerusalem only his friends knew where he slept.
○ *Small group of pupils mimes sleeping on the floor.*

*Narrator*    While the friends slept, one named Judas crept away to meet the enemies of Jesus.
○ *One of the group stands and creeps away to meet a group of others, who mime handing money over to Judas.*

**Narrator**     For this money Judas would take Jesus's enemies to find Jesus and, when they found him, Judas would kiss Jesus.

O *Judas leads the group to where the others are sleeping. During this, Jesus and the disciples mime waking up, and then stand. Judas brings the two groups together and puts his arms around Jesus. Two pupils from the group with Judas step forward and lead Jesus away; the crowd follows. The disciples remain still for a moment, then leave in the opposite direction.*

**Narrator**     Jesus was taken to Pontius Pilate, the Roman ruler of Jerusalem, and trial. He was found guilty and sentenced to death by crucifixion.

O *Crowd leads Jesus across the room to where Pilate is seated. Jesus stands in front of Pilate. Crowd steps back, away from Jesus and Pilate.*

**Narrator**     Pilate thought that, as it was the Jewish custom to free a prisoner during the Feast of the Passover, the crowd might agree to free Jesus. But they shouted for Barabbas, a common criminal, to be freed instead.

O *Crowd shout:* Free Barabbas! Free Barabbas!

**Narrator**     After that, Jesus was led away by soldiers and made to carry a heavy wooden cross to a hill called Calvary. Here he was nailed to the cross and crucified.

O *Two pupils step forward from the crowd and lead Jesus away.*

**Narrator**     Jesus was resurrected (came back to life) three days' later and returned to meet his friends (called disciples).

Conclude the assembly by pointing out that over Easter, although Christians remember the crucifixion on Good Friday, they also remember Jesus's return to life on Easter Sunday. These events make this a very important time for Christians. If was mainly because of them that Jesus's companions, the disciples, went on to found the Christian religion. The Narrator's statements could be replaced by the appropriate verses from *Matthew's Gospel, chapters 26 and 27.*

**Related assemblies**     None

# Easter traditions

**Theme**   The origins of Easter traditions

**Date**   Any time, a few weeks before Easter

**Materials**   None

**Assembly organization**   Start by asking what is the first tradition that comes into pupils' minds when they think of Easter. (You might need to explain what you mean by 'tradition'.)

Collect some answers from the pupils. Move on to say that you want to look at some of the Easter traditions and where they come from. Explain that the name Easter probably comes from the Anglo-Saxon word *Eostre*, which was the name for the pagan goddess of spring. Mention that in pre-Christian times, festivals were held to celebrate the start of spring.

Move on to outline some of the following traditions:

**Easter eggs**   Before the days of Jesus people would give eggs to each other as part of springtime festivals. These eggs would be dyed or painted fancy colours. So it was quite natural for eggs to be incorporated into the Christian Easter festival.

**Easter bunny**   The hare was always part of the springtime festivals to the pagan goddess, and in many countries today, the Easter hare traditionally brings children their Easter eggs. In America hares are often called rabbits and this may be the origin of the 'Easter Bunny'.

**Easter cards**   Cards are usually decorated with eggs, chicks, hares or rabbits, and have been sent for many years as part of Easter celebrations.

**Easter bonnets**   It has always been customary for people to wear new clothes on Easter Sunday and this idea is continued by Easter parades and Easter bonnets. Prior to this assembly, pupils could have been encouraged to make their own Easter bonnets to be worn as part of a parade in the assembly.

**Hot cross buns**   Ask the pupils what else is traditional to eat at Easter, in addition to Easter eggs. Bring out the answer: hot cross buns.

Go on to point out that cakes with a cross baked on them have long been part of springtime festivals, even before the time of Jesus. Today hot cross buns should be eaten on Good Friday; the cross baked on them reminds Christians of Jesus's suffering on the cross.

You might also like to mention a less widely known tradition:

**Easter games**   As Easter has always been a time of rejoicing for Christians, it has also been customary to play lively games. People in the southern part of England played marbles between Ash Wednesday and Good Friday (which was called Marble Day). Easter Monday was also referred to as Ball Monday because it was traditional to play all sorts of ball games.

Today many of the traditional games have been replaced by football, but in Hallaton (Leicestershire) the game of bottle kicking is still played.

You could conclude the assembly by explaining to the pupils that Easter is the most important festival for Christians. It is a time when they remember Jesus's death and resurrection to save people from their sins.

Go on to tell the pupils some of the significant dates in the Easter calendar:

- Palm Sunday, which commemorates Jesus's last journey to Jerusalem
- Good Friday, which commemorates Jesus's trial and crucifixion
- Easter Sunday, which commemorates the resurrection.

**Related assemblies**   None

# The Christmas story

**Theme** Christmas

**Date** Any time in the last week of term before Christmas

**Materials** Three small parcels
Small doll wrapped in a blanket
Large box on a chair (to act as the manger)
Five chairs

**Assembly organization** It will be necessary to rehearse the following scenes in advance of the assembly date.

At the start of the assembly get the pupils into their appropriate positions.

Begin the assembly by explaining that it will illustrate the Christmas story. Christmas is a very important time for Christians, as it celebrates the birth of Jesus. Jesus's life, death and resurrection are the bases of the Christian religion.

**Narrator** About 2000 years ago a very powerful Roman Emperor, Caesar Augustus, ordered that everyone in the Empire should return to the city of their parents, to be taxed. Joseph's family came from Bethlehem so he and his wife, Mary, had to travel there.

O *Mary (seated on the chair) mimes riding on a donkey. Joseph mimes walking alongside the donkey.*

**Narrator** This was a hard journey, particularly as Mary was expecting a baby. Mary and Joseph arrived at Bethlehem and they went from inn to inn trying to find a room.

O *Mary remains seated while Joseph walks around miming knocking on doors and being turned away by the inn keepers.*

**Narrator** Eventually Mary and Joseph came to an inn which was full but the inn keeper said they could stay in the stable.

O *Inn keeper mimes showing Mary and Joseph round to the stable. Mary and Joseph sit down on two chairs by the manger. (The doll should already be in the box on a chair.)*

**Narrator** In fields nearby, shepherds were looking after their sheep when suddenly an angel appeared before them.

O *A small group of shepherds, sitting on the floor, mime keeping warm by a fire. Angel stands up from behind a chair. Shepherds look worried.*

**Narrator**   The angel said that in Bethlehem a child had been born who would become a king and saviour. The angel told the shepherds to go down into the town and see the baby.
O *Angel sits down out of sight behind the chair again. Shepherds stand and walk over to where Mary and Joseph are seated.*

**Narrator**   Once the angel had gone, the shepherds stood and went down into the town to find the baby.
O *Shepherds gather around the manger; Mary picks up the doll and holds it in her arms for the shepherds to see. After this the shepherds should leave and Mary can place the doll back in the box.*

**Narrator**   Also, far away in the East, three Wise Men saw a bright new star which they knew was the sign of a new king being born.
O *The Wise Men point upwards and look at the star. Wise Men pick up their parcels and walk towards the star and the stable where Mary and Joseph are seated.*

**Narrator**   Once the Wise Men saw the star, they followed it until they found the stable. Here they gave presents to the baby.
O *Wise Men walk towards Mary and Joseph and lay their presents on the floor in front of the manger. Once again Mary picks up the doll and holds it in her arms for the Wise Men to see. (After this Mary can again place the doll back in the box.) The Wise Men leave.*

Conclude the assembly by asking the pupils if they know what the three gifts were. You could also mention that the Wise Men were believed to have arrived some time after the birth. This is celebrated at Epiphany. The Narrator's statements could be replaced by the appropriate verses from *Luke 2, 1–16* and *Matthew 2, 1–12.*

**Related assemblies**   None

# Christmas cards and all that

**Theme**  British Christmas traditions

**Date**  Any time during December

**Materials**  None

**Assembly organization**  Start the assembly by asking the pupils what traditional things they think of at Christmas time, other than giving presents.

Go on to outline some of our Christmas traditions. Here are some you might like to use:

*Christmas cards*  The tradition of sending Christmas cards probably only dates back to 1843 when Sir Henry Cole had special hand-painted cards made. The cards contained the words, 'A Merry Christmas and a Happy New Year to You'.

*Christmas decorations*  The tradition of decorations extends back to Roman times, when evergreens such as holly would be brought into the house as decoration for the winter festivals.

*Christmas tree*  The Christmas tree is a German tradition. It is thought to have been brought to this country in about 1841 by Queen Victoria's husband, Prince Albert, although some Germans living in England had Christmas trees in their homes as early as 1829. Queen Victoria and Prince Albert popularized the tree as a central part of a family Christmas.

*Christmas turkey*  Before turkey became popular people would have bustard, goose or cockerel as a special part of their Christmas meal. In the households of the rich they ate peacock or swan.

*Chocolate log (Yule log)*  Today's chocolate log (Yule log) is an edible representation of another traditional Christmas event: the bringing of a large log into the house and its burning through the Christmas period. In houses with a large fireplace the Yule log could burn on until Twelfth Night.

**Boxing Day**    The day after Christmas is traditionally called Boxing Day. One belief as to how it got its name relates to the Christmas tradition of leaving alms (poor) boxes in churches over the Christmas period. These boxes were opened on Christmas Day and the money they contained, called the 'Box money', given out the day after Christmas.

Conclude the assembly by asking the pupils what is the main thing that they think of when they think of Christmas. Bring out the answer: Christmas presents.

Go on to talk about the commercialization of Christmas; how it is seen by many people as a time of year to make money, and that by concentrating on making and spending money we are forgetting the original meaning of Christmas.

Ask the pupils what Christians remember at Christmas. Bring out the answer: The birth of Jesus.

End the assembly by reminding the pupils that although Christmas is a time when they give and receive presents they should not forget that it is also the Christian celebration of the birth of Jesus.

**Related**    None
**assemblies**

# Pancake Day

**Theme**  Traditions behind Shrove Tuesday

**Date**  On Shrove Tuesday or in the week before

**Materials**  Three pancakes (which can be made the day before)
Three frying pans

**Assembly organization**  Start the assembly by explaining to the pupils that you want to look at the reasons for Shrove Tuesday. Ask what is the other name for Shrove Tuesday. Bring out the answer: Pancake Day. Explain that one of the Shrove Tuesday traditions is to hold pancake races and that today you want to have your own pancake race.

Ask for three volunteers and explain how to run your pancake race. (It is suggested that the race is based more on the skill of flipping pancakes than on speed.) Hold the pancake race; you might want to repeat it with another group of volunteers.

After the races, ask the pupils if they can tell you what pancakes are made from. Bring out the answer: Eggs, flour, milk, salt, and fat for frying.

Explain that, traditionally, these foods were not to be eaten during Lent, which is the forty days and nights immediately before Easter. So, rather than being thrown away, they were made into pancakes and eaten on Shrove Tuesday, the day before the start of Lent. You might also like to mention that the first day of Lent is called Ash Wednesday.

If you wish you could further explain that the name 'Ash Wednesday' comes from an early Christian Church practice. Penitents (which you could define as people who regret doing wrong and wish to be forgiven) were made to wear sack cloth and place ashes on their heads. This tradition is continued in some churches by marking crosses on the forehead using ashes from the previous year's palm crosses.

Go on to point out that the forty days of Lent represents the time Jesus spent in the wilderness. (You might wish to say more about what happened to Jesus during his time in the wilderness. See *Luke 4, 1–13*.)

Make it clear that pancake races are only one Shrove Tuesday tradition. You could then go on to mention other traditions and any local customs. For example:

***Shrovetide football***  This is a game played in Ashbourne in Derbyshire. The goals are three miles apart, separated by a stream. The game is played by two teams: Up'ards and Down'ards, depending on which side of the stream the players live.

Conclude by telling pupils that it is also traditional for Christians to give up things for the period of Lent (to remember the time Jesus spent in the desert). Suggest that they might like to give up something for Lent, e.g. sweets or chocolate, and that any money saved be given to a charity.

**Related assemblies**  None

# Chinese New Year

**Theme**   Chinese New Year and the story of the twelve animals

**Date**   In the week of the Chinese New Year

**Materials**   Large world map
A4 size paper with twelve animal names on:

| RAT | DRAGON | MONKEY |
|---|---|---|
| OX | SNAKE | COCK |
| TIGER | HORSE | DOG |
| RABBIT | RAM | PIG |

***Chinese New Year animal sequence***

| Rat | Ox | Tiger | Rabbit | Dragon | Snake |
|---|---|---|---|---|---|
| Horse | Ram | Monkey | Cock | Dog | Pig |

**Assembly organization**   **S**tart the assembly by asking for twelve volunteers to hold up the animal names.

Ask the pupils if they can tell you the connection between the animal names. Bring out the answer: They are the names of the Chinese New Years. Go on to point out to pupils where China is on the world map.

Next ask the pupils which animal year it is now in the Chinese calendar.

| 1995 | 1996 | 1997 | 1998 | 1999 |
|---|---|---|---|---|
| Pig | Rat | Ox | Tiger | Rabbit |

You could continue by asking them what year it will be next year.

Then explain to the pupils the origins of the sequence of the animals. Either by yourself or by organizing a small group of pupils, read the story of how the animals' order was decided. (See additional notes on page 20.)

Go on to talk about some Chinese traditions for New Year:

- No one goes to sleep (little children are discouraged from dozing off) as it is believed it shortens your life if you are not awake for the arrival of New Year's Day.

- When the New Year arrives the head of the family gives all the young members of the family traditional gifts called *lai see* (lucky money) to bring them good fortune for the year to come.

- The first day of the New Year is set aside for worship and visiting relatives. When visiting it is customary to wear new clothes.

The following are some other facts about China that you might like to mention:

- Most famous thing built by the Chinese: the Great Wall of China.
  The Great Wall was built to defend China from hostile tribes. It is the only structure built by people which can be seen from space.

- Most famous animal: Giant Panda.
  The Giant Panda lives in areas of western China and there are only about 1000 left alive.

End the assembly by suggesting that on Chinese New Year's Day pupils might like to greet their parents and friends with a traditional Chinese greeting: *Kung hey fat choi*. This means 'Wishing you to prosper'.

**Related assemblies**  None

**Additional notes**

***Order of the twelve animals in the Chinese calendar***

The order of the animals can be explained by a legend which goes as follows. The rat, ox, tiger, rabbit, dragon, snake, horse, ram, monkey, cock, dog and pig agreed to hold a swimming race across a river to decide whose year should come first.

The animals entered the water and started swimming. The rat cunningly jumped on to the ox's back, as it was the best swimmer. When the ox reached the other side of the river the rat jumped off on to the land first.

From then on the years have started with the year of the rat, followed by the other animals in the order they finished the race: ox, tiger, rabbit, dragon, snake, horse, ram, monkey, cock, dog and pig.

(When the sequence of animals is read out the rest of the pupils could be encouraged to say them at the same time.)

# Ramadan

**Theme**   The Muslim celebration of Ramadan

**Date**   At a time just before the start of the month of Ramadan

**Materials**   None

**Assembly organization**   Begin the assembly by explaining that you want to talk about a Muslim celebration which is soon to begin. Many people in this country and around the world will be observing this special time.

Ask the pupils if they can tell you the name of this special Muslim month. Bring out the answer: Ramadan.

Go on to explain that Ramadan is a very important time for Muslims. It celebrates the time when Muslims believe the prophet Muhammad was visited by the Angel Jibril (Gabriel). Jibril gave Muhammad messages from God which were later written down in the Qur'an (the Muslim holy book).

Ask the pupils if they know the name given to God by Muslims. Bring out the answer: Allah.

Ask the pupils what special things Muslims have to do during the month of Ramadan. Bring out the answer: They have to fast (go without all food and water) during the hours of daylight and that they have to do this for one full lunar month. Go on to explain that Muslims do this because they believe it is Allah's will and that it will teach them to lead a good life.

Explain that children under the age of twelve, pregnant women, the sick and elderly do not have to fast. They are all people who, for one reason or another, would not be able to go without food and water for such a long period.

As well as fasting during Ramadan, Muslims are encouraged to pray more frequently. (They would normally pray five times a day.) They should also try to read all of the Qur'an during this month. Remind the pupils that the Qur'an is the Muslim holy book which is believed to contain the words of Allah, as given to Muhammad by the angel Jibril.

Next point out to the pupils that the Muslim

calendar is determined by the cycles of the moon and that Ramadan is the ninth month. This means that the exact time of Ramadan in the western calendar changes each year. Fasting is particularly demanding and requires great determination when it falls during the long hours of daylight during summer.

Explain that the exact time at which daylight begins and ends is not an easy thing to decide. (It stays light after the sun has set and becomes light before the sun rises.) To solve this problem Muslims in many parts of the world listen for the call to prayer (adhan) from the minaret. Today many also listen to announcements given out by radio and television.

Explain to the pupils that during Ramadan Muslims will often eat a light meal before sunrise and then end their fast after the sun has gone down with a date or maybe a drink of water. Then, before their evening meal, they pray. Go on to say that Ramadan ends in the evening after about one month with the sighting of the new moon. The ending of Ramadan is called *Id-ul-Fitr*. The morning after the new moon has been sighted Muslims put on new clothes and go to the mosque to pray.

You might like to conclude the assembly by briefly outlining the five important parts of the Muslim faith. They are called the Five Pillars:

1  **Faith** (the belief in Allah as the one God and Muhammad as his prophet)
2  **Prayer (Muslims should pray five times a day)**
3  **Alms giving** (donating money to the poor)
4  **Fasting** (during Ramadan)
5  **Pilgrimage** (to Makkah)

End the assembly by saying that you hope the pupils now have a better understanding of Ramadan, which Muslims all around the world will be observing over the next few weeks.

**Related assemblies**    None

# Rama and Sita

**Theme** The story of Divali (sometimes spelt Diwali)

**Date** Just before the Festival of Divali, in October or November

**Materials** Eleven large sheets of paper with the following sentences on them. You may want only to put the information inside the square brackets; the rest you can use at the appropriate time.

[The young prince Rama visited a nearby country.] Rama was the oldest son of the King Dasharatha who had three other sons.

[Rama picked up the bow and strung it, but it broke.] While away in a nearby country, Rama met Sita. To marry her he had to string her father's bow.

[Rama and Sita were married.] After the marriage they returned to Ayodhya to be with Rama's father.

[Rama, Sita and Lakshmana (Rama's brother) were forced to leave Ayodhya.] One day when the king was old and near to death, he was persuaded to grant one of his wives a wish. As she wanted her son Bharata to become king, she asked that Rama and Sita should be sent away for fourteen years. They left to live in the forest, and Lakshmana went with them.

[The old king, Dasharatha, died.] After the king's death, Bharata's mother said he was now to become king. But Bharata said he would not be king. Instead, he would go into the forest and bring back Rama.

[Prince Bharata went into the forest and found Rama.] Rama said he would not return as he had promised his father he would stay away fourteen years. Prince Bharata asked for Rama's golden sandals and returned home.

[Prince Bharata placed the golden sandals on the throne.] When he returned, Bharata said he would look after the people until Rama returned, but he would not sit on the throne.

[Ravana captured Sita and took her away.] Ravana was

a wicked ten-headed demon who took Sita away while Rama and Lakshmana were out hunting. Sita refused to marry Ravana so he imprisoned her in a castle on a far away island.

[Rama and Lakshmana returned from hunting and could not find Sita.] They were told where to find Sita by Hanuman, king of the monkeys.

[Rama, Hanuman and their friends went to fight Ravana.] In the battle that followed, Rama killed Ravana.

[Rama found Sita and they returned to Ayodhya.] When they returned, riding on an elephant, it was dark so all the people put lights outside their homes.

**Assembly organization**

At the start of the assembly collect eleven volunteers and give each one a piece of paper to hold up. Make sure the statements are not shown in the correct sequence.

Tell the pupils that the statements they can see are part of a famous story from India, and that it is one that Hindus celebrate at this time of year.

Ask pupils if they can tell you the name of the festival. Bring out the answer: Divali. Go on to explain that the story comes from a famous Indian book called the *Ramayana*, which is a book sacred to Hindus.

Next say that you would like, with the pupils' help, to sort the sentences into the correct sequence and to tell the story of Divali. Work through the sequencing exercise with the pupils (which they should be able to do either because they know the story or by using simple logic). As each sentence is put in the correct order, add the additional information provided.

Conclude the assembly by pointing out that many people today celebrate the Festival of Divali (Festival of Lights) by having little lights in their houses. They do this to remember the time when the evil demon Ravana was killed by Rama and good conquered evil. These lights are reminders of the ones used to greet Rama and Sita, to guide them back home.

**Related assemblies**

None

# Our effect on others and the world around us

These assemblies provide a variety of ways to encourage pupils to think of others less fortunate than themselves and of their responsibility towards the environment and the world around them. There are also a number of assemblies providing alternative approaches to the topic of bullying.

| Assembly | Theme |
| --- | --- |
| Share and share alike | *Sharing with others* |
| Feed the world | *World poverty and starvation* |
| The widow's offering | *Give what you can to charity* |
| It's not the size of the gift but the thought that counts | *Giving to others at Christmas* |
| The power of speech | *Positive use of language* |
| Sticks and stones | *Name calling as a form of bullying* |
| You don't know you're born | *Thinking of others* |
| What you want isn't what you need | *The difference between needs and wants* |
| Two wrongs don't make a right | *What to do if you're bullied* |
| The life of the bully | *No one wins when people bully* |
| Litter | *Litter as a hazard, and recycling* |
| Switch it off | *Energy conservation, and pollution* |
| It's their world too | *Conservation of habitats and species* |

# Share and share alike

**Theme** Sharing with others

**Date** No specific date

**Materials** Packet of individually wrapped sweets (Before the assembly count how many sweets the packet contains.)

**Assembly organization** From the assembly ask for as many volunteers as there are sweets in the packet, and get them to line up at the front. Open the packet and explain that you intend to share out the sweets among the pupils who have volunteered to help.

Start at one end of the line and give a few of the pupils one sweet each. Then start to give the pupils two sweets. Finally give one pupil three of four sweets and give the next one the rest of the packet (count how many are left in the packet so everyone knows how many the pupil is being given). Turn to the rest of the pupil volunteers and apologize for the fact that there are no sweets left for them.

Ask the rest of the assembly what they think of the way you have shared out the sweets.

Bring out the answer: It's unfair. Ask them to explain why it's unfair. Bring out the answer: Because not everyone has been given a sweet. Ask the pupils if they've heard the saying: 'Share and share alike'. Ask them what they think this saying means.

Next talk about how you should have shared out the sweets. Turn to the volunteers and redistribute the sweets so that all the pupils have one sweet each. Let the volunteers sit down and allow them to eat their sweets.

Go on to relate this illustration to how the Earth's wealth is not equally shared. The western world is represented by the pupil who had the rest of the sweets. Britain is part of the western world, which has used the largest share of the world's resources, and has more food than it needs. Explain that the pupils with no sweets represent people in Third World countries, many of whom are always hungry and may starve to death.

Go on to ask the pupils if their parents talk about starving people in other parts of the world when they leave food on their plates. Explain it isn't as simple as the redistribution of the sweets. We cannot just send our spare food over to these countries.

You might like to talk about how it is necessary to send food during a crisis but how this is not a long-term solution. Some reasons why, which you might like to outline are:

- people do not like to depend on charity all their life
- sending free food can remove the market for local farmers to sell their food, restricting their ability to develop and help themselves.

Conclude by suggesting that, in this case, one way to share and share alike is to donate money to the charities that support people in Third World countries. These help them to grow their own food.

**Related assemblies**  Feed the world

# Feed the world

**Theme**  World poverty and starvation

**Date**  No specific date

**Materials**  OHP 1: Feed the world
OHP 2: What money can buy
Overhead projector and screen

**Assembly organization**  Start the assembly by asking the pupils if any of them missed their breakfast. Ask any pupils who did how they feel. Bring out the answer: 'Hungry'. (If you get the answer 'starving' go straight on to talk about people who really are starving.) Next ask the pupils if anyone missed their evening meal as well. (It is hoped that no one missed both meals.) Then ask the pupils how they think they might feel if they had not eaten a meal all day. Bring out the answer: 'Starving'. Go on to explain that today you want to talk about people who might not have had anything to eat for a whole week.

Put up the screen OHP 1. Uncover and show only diagram 1. Explain that this diagram shows that the world can grow more than enough food to feed its whole population. You could go on to highlight a number of points at this stage:

1  excess food is consumed or wasted by the western world, i.e. most of us eat more than we need and often leave food on our plates
2  there are stock piles of food in the west
3  good ground is used for the growth of tobacco and other cash crops when it could be used to grow food.

Or you may prefer to move on to the next diagram.

Uncover diagram 2. Explain that in the world today, one child dies of starvation every two seconds. Time five periods of two seconds and, after each one, cross out a figure. (This point could be further emphasized if a row of five pupils stood at the front and after each two seconds, one of them sat down.)

Uncover diagram 3. Explain that 50 per cent (half) of the world's population does not have access to the clean drinking water we take for granted. Go on to say how, in many countries, water doesn't come from a tap but has to be carried from an open well.

Move on to say that, of course, this shortage of food and clean water is not our fault. It wouldn't help for us just to cut down on the food we eat because the food cannot simply be sent to these countries. Ask the pupils how they think they could help. Bring out the answer: By giving money to charity.

Put up on the screen OHP 2. Start by uncovering the £2 sign and explain that £2 given to charity can buy enough vaccine to protect approximately 60 children in some parts of the world against measles, diphtheria and whooping cough. Uncover the £3 sign and explain that £3 could buy approximately 60 packets of rehydration solution for children suffering from diarrhoea. Go on the explain that many children in Third World countries get diarrhoea from the dirty water they drink and that without these packets of rehydration solution they would die. Finally, uncover the £5 sign and explain that this amount would provide enough seed for farmers to feed their family for approximately one year. Go on to say that this is a better way to prevent starvation than just sending our excess food. It helps people in the Third World to grow their own food and to be self sufficient.

Conclude the assembly by pointing out that they, of course, don't have to give money to charities. But perhaps sometimes they could think of other people and go without the occasional snack. They could give the money they would have spent to a charity instead.

**Related assembly**    Share and share alike

## OHP 1: Feed the world

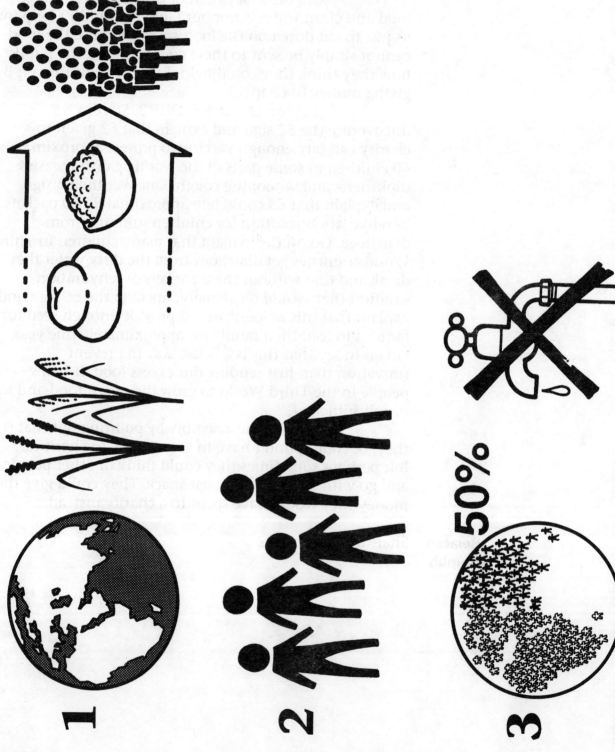

OHP 2: What money can buy

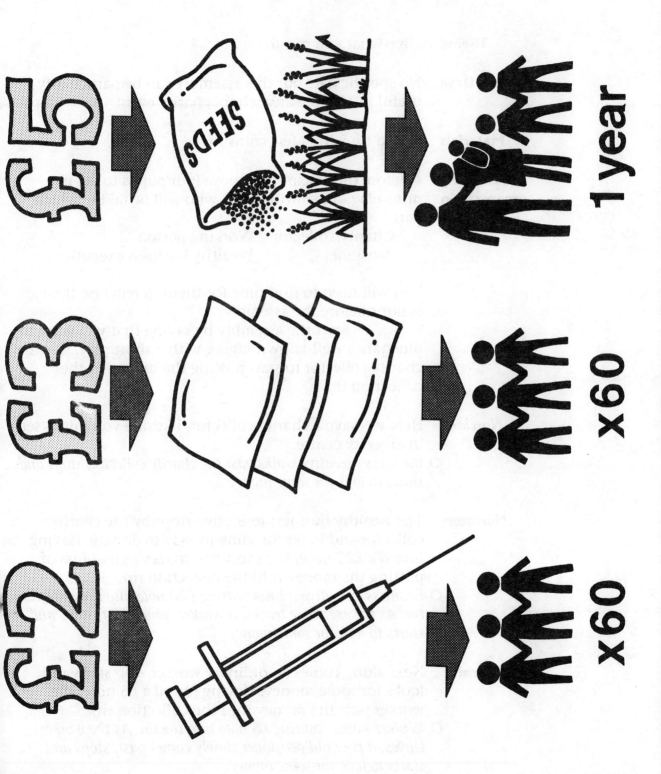

# The widow's offering

**Theme**   Give what you can to charity

**Date**   No specific date but this assembly can be particularly useful just before any school charity event

**Materials**   Sealed tin with a few coins in it

**Assembly organization**   Before the assembly, choose four pupils to act in a mini-play. Agree with them who will be taking which part:

| | |
|---|---|
| Charity collector | Working person |
| Pensioner | Wealthy business executive |

You will need to find time for them to rehearse their actions before the assembly.

Start the assembly by saying that you want to illustrate a well-known saying with a short play. Get the charity collector to start rattling the money in the collection tin.

**Narrator**   Here we have a charity collector, like one you might see in any city centre.

O *Business executive walks past the charity collector, stops and starts to look for some money.*

**Narrator**   The wealthy business executive stops by the charity collector and looks for some money to donate. Having found a £20 note, the executive makes a great fuss of putting the money into the collection tin.

O *Business executive mimes putting £20 note into the collection tin. As the executive leaves, a worker comes past, stops and starts to look for some money.*

**Narrator**   Next along comes an ordinary worker who stops and looks for some money. Having found a £5 note, the worker puts the money into the collection tin.

O *Worker mimes putting £5 note into the tin. As the worker leaves, a poor old pensioner slowly comes past, stops and starts to look for some money.*

**Narrator**   Here we see a rather poor old pensioner, looking for some money. Having found 50 pence, the pensioner quietly slips the money into the tin.

O *Pensioner mimes putting 50 pence into the collecting tin.*

Ask the pupils which of these three people has been the most generous. Hopefully they will say the pensioner. You can then talk about how the pensioner is probably giving money that is needed to buy something essential. The others, however, are likely to be giving money from their spare cash, which they don't really need. They probably won't miss it.

Ask the pupils if they know which saying this assembly illustrates. Bring out the answer: 'It's not the size of the gift but the thought that counts.' (If the saying has not been introduced before to the pupils, you may need to help them.) You can then go on to explain that whenever you give a donation to a charity, what matters is not how much you give but that you give as much as you can.

You may want to conclude by asking the pupils where this story originally came from. It is one of the stories Jesus told (see *Luke 21, 1–4*) and is called the Widow's Offering.

**Related assembly**    It's not the size of the gift but the thought that counts

# It's not the size of the gift but the thought that counts

**Theme** Giving to others at Christmas

**Date** In the weeks before Christmas

**Materials** Twelve pieces of A4 size card. Each card should have one word from the phrase 'It's not the size of the gift but the thought that counts' written on it. On the reverse side of the card, with the words in the correct sequence, write small numbers one to twelve.

Eight pieces of A4 size card, prepared as above, using the saying, 'It is better to give than to receive'

**Assembly organization** From the assembly as a whole or from your own form collect twelve volunteers. Give each pupil one of the cards for the first saying. (Make certain the words are not in the correct order.) Ask the volunteers to read out the words on their cards. The words can be shown at the same time.

Explain to the assembly that these words represent a well known saying and ask if anyone thinks that they could rearrange the words to reveal it. Anyone who feels they know the saying can then come forward and attempt to arrange the words into the correct order. (Staff could also be asked to come forward and try.)

When volunteers come forward to rearrange the words into a saying (by moving the pupils) the words should be concealed making this a memory exercise (ensure the numbers cannot be seen). After each attempt, the pupils should read out the word on their card. This can produce some unusual sayings and can prove entertaining.

After a number of tries, reveal the saying by asking pupils to arrange themselves into the correct order. Now ask them to read out their word.

Next collect another eight volunteers and repeat the exercise with the second saying.

Conclude the assembly by pointing out the meaning behind the two sayings:

- you do not have to give an expensive present;

sometimes a small home-made one can have more value to it

- as Christmas approaches you should not just be thinking of what you want, but should also be asking what other people would like.

Continue by suggesting that at this time of the year, when parents are very busy, perhaps one of the best presents they could give would be to help around the house. They could offer to do some jobs, such as fetching the shopping or washing up.

**Related assembly**   The widow's offering

# The power of speech

**Theme**  Positive use of language

**Date**  No specific date

**Materials**  None

**Assembly organization**  Start the assembly by talking to the pupils about what ability sets humans apart from other animals. They may reply 'making tools' which is correct, but guide them towards the answer: Only humans have developed complex language (speech). Talk about how other animals have developed types of language but not the complicated speech that we have. Animals have developed the ability to communicate through signs and gestures, which humans can also do.

Look at some of the signs and gestures that humans use. Some examples might be:

- shaking your head (no)
- nodding your head (yes)
- pointing at a child and gesturing for them to come out.

Talk about the limitations of these types of gesture – how they are not always clear and can only communicate simple ideas. Move on to talk about how complicated our speech can be in comparison with signs and gestures.

Next you could start to talk about how some of the things people have said (or are reputed to have said) have become famous and have been remembered for many years. Some examples might be:

- 'We are not amused' – Queen Victoria
- 'There's time to win the game and thrash the Spaniards' (believed to have been said) – Sir Francis Drake
- 'England expects every man to do his duty' (This would also have been signalled to the other ships) – Admiral Lord Nelson
- 'You turn if you want to. The lady's not for turning' – Margaret Thatcher
- 'I came, I saw, I conquered' – Julius Caesar

- 'Never in the field of human conflict has so much been owed by so many, to so few' – Winston Churchill
- 'It's one small step for man. One giant leap for mankind' – Neil Armstrong
- 'Let them eat cake' – Marie-Antoinette
- 'You'll like this. Not a lot!' – Paul Daniels
- 'Not like that – just like that!' – Tommy Cooper

Read out each saying and ask pupils if they know who said it.

Now move on to talk about how sometimes things are remembered because they are funny. Relate this to the last two sayings. This is especially true of radio and television commentators who have to talk continuously and often not from a prepared script. Some examples might be:

- 'Dusty Hare kicked nineteen of the seventeen points'
- 'I'm speaking from a deserted and virtually empty Crucible Theatre'
- 'He's going up and down like a metronome'
- 'This boy swims like a greyhound'
- 'He is now set up to pot the black (for those you watching in black and white) which is just behind the pink.'

Read out each statement; you might need to explain some of them a little to help the pupils see the funny side.

Conclude by talking about the power of speech and how things people say can be remembered for years. Point out that, regrettably, not everyone uses the power of speech to do good; some people use speech to hurt others. Introduce the idea that some uses of language are unacceptable. Examples might be:

- name calling
- swearing at people
- gossiping about people.

End by talking about these being unacceptable uses of language and how we should avoid using the power of speech in this way.

**Related assembly**   Sticks and stones

# Sticks and stones

**Theme**   Name calling as a form of bullying

**Date**   No specific date

**Materials**   Small collection of:

- sticks
- stones
- bones (most science departments should be able to provide these)
- seven pieces of card with the following words written on them:
  sticks stones bones break hurt words me

**Assembly organization**   Arrange your items at random on a table at the front of the hall. Start the assembly by holding up various objects from your collection. Talk about putting the objects from your collection into groups or sets. Get the pupils to place the objects into the following sets in this order:

     sticks
     stones
     bones
     words

Having produced the sets with the given names, ask the pupils if they can tell you which saying this reminds them of. (If they have any difficulty, use the collection of words in their correct sequence.) Bring out the answer: 'Sticks and stones may break my bones but words will never hurt me'. Talk about the meaning of this saying. Ask the pupils how they might feel if they were being called names. Some answers to bring out might be:

     upset       lonely
     sad         frightened
     hurt

Move on to talk to the pupils about how they should deal with name calling. Some points you might like to bring out are:

- The first time someone calls them names, it's worth ignoring them to start with (but not if the things are particularly nasty and upset them).
- If someone is regularly calling them names or saying

nasty things, they should report it to an adult (for example, parents or a teacher) so they can get it stopped.

Ask the pupils what is one thing they should not do if someone is calling them names. Bring out the answer: You should not call them names back. Ask the pupils what could happen if they did call them names back. Bring out the answer: It could lead to a fight.

Explain to the pupils that, as a bystander, they could either suggest that the bully stop calling names or they could be nice to the person being bullied and try to find other ways to help them. Remind the pupils that this is especially true for someone who does not have many other friends.

Conclude the assembly by reminding the pupils of the saying: 'Do unto others, as you would have them do unto you'. Explain its meaning and point out that no one likes other people being nasty to them. Even the people who call names get upset and soon want it stopped if others start calling them names.

**Related assembly**    The power of speech

# You don't know you're born

**Theme**  Thinking of others

**Date**  No specific date

**Materials**  Three small cards with the following sentences written on them:

- One day I fell asleep and when I woke up the rats had eaten my bread and cheese.
- I'm a trapper in the pit. It doesn't tire me, but I have to work in the dark and I'm scared.
- My clothes are wet through almost all day long. I am very tired when I get home at night. I fall asleep sometimes before I get washed.

OHP: The trapper (using page 43)
Overhead projector and screen

**Assembly organization**  **B**efore the assembly, collect three volunteers from your form to read out the information on the cards.

Start the assembly by asking the pupils to complete these sayings:

- 'You have never had it so . . .'
- 'You do not know how luck . . .'
- 'You don't know you are . . .'
- 'The grass is always greener on . . .'

Explain that these sayings are all to do with the fact that we tend to look at the bad side of our lives and not at how good things are. Go on to explain that in today's assembly you want to try to show the pupils how lucky they are. To do this you want to look at the life they might have had just over a hundred years ago, when they could have found themselves working down the mines.

Ask the pupils if any of them got up early this morning. Ask them what time they got up. Go on to say that if they had worked down the mines they would have worked the following day:

4.00 a.m.   Get up
6.00 a.m.   Start work

| 8.00 a.m. | Breakfast |
| 8.30 a.m. | Back to work |
| 12.00 noon | Stop for lunch |
| 2.00 p.m. | Afternoon work |
| 7.30 p.m. | Stop work |
| 8.00 p.m. | Go to bed |

They would have worked this routine six or seven days a week. Children as young as five worked these hours down the mines. They had a job called 'trapping'.

Put the OHP up on the screen – the picture of a trapper. Tell pupils that a trapper would spend up to twelve hours sitting like this in a coal mine in the dark. The trapper's job was to open a door as older children pushed the trucks full of coal up to the surface. Say that you want the pupils to listen to what three trappers thought of their job down the mines. Ask the three pupils to read out their sentences.

Emphasize the trapper's predicament further by suggesting that we would all have been frightened if, at the age of five, we spent hours sitting in the dark, with our clothes soaking wet and rats running about around our feet. Of course, as the children got older, they were lucky – or were they? Older boys and girls had to push heavy coal waggons up to the surface of the coal mine.

Mines were not the only places children worked long hours. Some children worked in factories. They were often so tired that they fell asleep and could not do their work properly. One employer said of these tired children: 'They are very careless working on the machines and lose their fingers, but they seldom lose their hand.' What a caring employer he was. Other children might not hurt themselves but produce work which was not very good. If they did they would be beaten with horse whips, belts, hammers or anything heavy that was to hand.

You could also go on to talk about children who swept chimneys.

Conclude this part of the assembly by saying how lucky everyone in the hall is. Those nineteenth-century children had a very rough life and were cruelly treated. But, of course, all that is in the past, children do not live like that today. Do they?

Oh yes they do! There are parts of the world where children are taken away from their homes and made to work hard for long hours. In some parts of the world children starve to death.

Finally, point out that children are still suffering around the world today. Instead of looking at the things we wish to have, we should look at how lucky we are. Conclude with the saying: 'Count your blessings'.

**Related assembly**    What you want isn't what you need

## OHP: The trapper

# What you want isn't what you need

**Theme**    The difference between needs and wants

**Date**    No specific date

**Materials**    Two pieces of A4 paper with the word 'Need' written on one and 'Want' on the other
Two large pieces of paper with the following definitions of needs and wants:

- To wish for something necessary

- To wish to have something

Five small pieces of paper with the following sentences written on them, to be read out by pupils:
**1** I need that car.
**2** What we need is a good holiday.
**3** You need a hair cut.
**4** I need a drink.
**5** We need a new video.

**Assembly organization**    **B**efore the assembly or at the beginning, arrange for a number of pupils to hold up the 'need', 'want' signs and their meanings, and to read out the statements.

Start by asking the pupils to hold up the 'need' and 'want' signs then, separately, ask the pupils to hold up the meanings. Ask the rest of the pupils to match the words and their correct meanings. After this, ask them to suggest the difference between the two meanings. In this bring out that a 'need' is something necessary.

Next ask the pupils to read out the series of statements one at a time and discuss if each one really represents a need. Before each statement you might like to put them into context, e.g.
**1** two small boys playing with cars
**2** a mother and father talking
**3** a father talking to his son
**4** a girl talking to her friends on a very hot day
**5** a man talking to his wife.

After each sentence discuss each statement and bring out

that only **4** really represents what could be a 'need'; all the rest are 'wants'.

Go on to talk about how today there are many things that people feel they need but which are not really necessary. You might like to ask the pupils if they feel a television is something they need, and go on to explain that life did exist before television was invented.

Go on to talk about which things are truly needed. Examples might be:

- food
- water
- air
- clothing (for warmth).

(Money is needed, of course, to buy three of these.)

Contrast these with other things we have which are luxuries (videos, televisions, computers, etc.). Conclude by pointing out how lucky we are and that in some parts of the world people have to struggle to get things they really need.

You could bring this assembly to an end by talking to the pupils about being greedy and wanting more and more things. You could refer them to the following story from the Bible: *Luke 12, 13–21*: the parable of the rich fool.

**Related assembly**   You don't know you're born

# Two wrongs don't make a right

**Theme**   What to do if you're bullied

**Date**   No specific date

**Materials**   One large piece of paper with these words written on it: wrong + wrong ≠ right

**Assembly organization**

**C**ollect one volunteer from the assembly and get them to hold up your sign. Ask the pupils what saying they think the sign represents. Bring out the answer: 'Two wrongs don't make a right.' Explain the meaning of the saying to the pupils and then ask them to suggest some types of wrong people could do to them, for example, stealing, hitting, name calling.

After talking about each example for a short time and relating it to the original saying, explain that you want to concentrate on two ways people could do wrong to them and what the pupils should do in each case.

**1 Calling people names**

Remind the pupils of the saying from the start of the assembly. Ask them what they should *not* do if anyone is calling them names. Bring out the answer: Call them names back. Go on to talk about what they could try doing instead. First of all, talk about ignoring the name calling. Make it clear that if it does not stop or if the names are particularly upsetting, they should try something else. For example, they can try staying away from the people calling the names. If it still doesn't stop, they should report it to an adult.

Emphasize that name calling is a form of bullying and as such is not acceptable.

**2 Hitting other people**

Again remind the pupils of the saying from the start of the assembly. Ask them what they should *not* do if someone is hitting (or kicking) them. Bring out the answer: Hit or kick back. Go on to point out that if they do hit back they could end up in a fight.

Tell the pupils that if they are hit or kicked (as long as it's only a minor incident) they should just walk away, no matter how difficult it may be. They can either report whatever happened to an adult or forget it. If they are hurt badly or the person keeps on hitting or kicking them, then they should definitely report it to an adult. Emphasize that no one should ever put up with being bullied and that reporting it is often the only way of getting it stopped.

You might also like to point out that, as a bystander, they can help the person who is being bullied. The easiest thing they can do is to go and tell an adult what they have seen. They could tell the person who is bullying to stop it, but this could mean the bully then picks on them, so it's often best just to report what they have seen.

Above all they should remember that they wouldn't like this to happen to them and remember to be nice to the bullied person.

**Related assembly**     The life of the bully

# The life of the bully

**Theme**  No one wins when people bully

**Date**  No specific date

**Materials**  None

**Assembly organization**  Before the assembly you need to work with a small group of volunteers from your form to produce a brief mini-play illustrating bullying. This should contain a bully and friend who pick on another pupil while other pupils are around to see what happens. You will need to carefully supervise the organization of this play to ensure it does not just glorify violence.

Start the assembly by explaining that you want everyone to watch a short play. Ask the volunteers to act out their play. At the end ask the assembly what the play illustrated and talk briefly about the incident of bullying it portrayed.

Next explain that you want to look at the consequences of bullying for the people involved. Ask pupils how they think the victim feels. Talk briefly about how upsetting it is to be bullied and how unpleasant it feels. Continue by explaining that it is not only the victim who is affected in these situations.

Ask the assembly how they think the bystanders feel in this situation. Bring out the answer: Concerned/worried that they might be next. Ask the assembly how they think the bully's friend feels. You may need to explain that he might feel a little worried too, as he has to do as the bully says or he might well get bullied himself. Go on to talk about how the bullying in the play would result in everyone involved feeling at least a little anxious.

Ask the assembly who is the only person in the play who does not seem to be upset by what is happening. Bring out the answer: The bully. Go on to explain that you want to look at how the bully's behaviour should really worry him/her.

First, ask the assembly if they have heard of the saying: 'You reap what you sow'. Ask what they think this means in the case of the bully. Bring out the answer:

When a bigger bully comes along, the original bully can be bullied him/herself. By bullying you get a reputation which means that one day you yourself may be bullied by a bigger bully.

Next remind the assembly how they thought the bully's friend might feel (remind them that bullies may well pick on their friends). Go on to talk about how the bully's friends probably wouldn't help the bully when he/she was in trouble and how they might look for better friends if they could.

Conclude that far from being happy and having no problems, the bully has a great deal to worry about. Bullies have few real friends and most probably will eventually be bullied themselves. (You might like to draw an analogy with the game 'I'm the king of the castle'; someone will surely come along one day and push him/her off.)

**Related assembly**    Two wrongs don't make a right

# Litter

| | |
|---|---|
| **Theme** | Litter as a hazard, and recycling |
| **Date** | No specific date |
| **Materials** | Prior to the assembly collect a large amount of clean pieces of litter and spread it around the assembly hall. (Do not use anything which could be a safety hazard.) |
| **Assembly organization** | |

**A**sk the pupils their opinion of the hall when they came in. Bring out the point that it was untidy and full of litter. Talk about the fact that the litter was composed of rubbish found around the school or local area. Ask the pupils why litter isn't normally left around and discuss how they feel about all the litter on the floor. Bring out:

1 It's not safe – broken glass can cut you.
2 Animals can choke on plastic bags or be trapped in four-pack holders.
3 Rubbish attracts rats and mice, and is a breeding place for germs. Consequently it can spread disease.
4 It is a form of pollution and spoils the environment.

(The pupils may need help to produce these answers.)

Talk to the pupils about the correct thing to do with litter and mention the various litter campaigns designed to encourage people to put litter in the bins. For example:

Keep Britain Tidy
Litter is ugly
Bin it, don't drop it.

After this you could talk about what else can be done with rubbish. Bring out the answer: Recycle it. (You can help by giving clues, for example by holding up paper or glass.)

Talk to the pupils about the advantages of recycling. Some points to bring out would be:

- recycling paper and card saves trees

- recycling all materials saves resources (recycling glass, which is made from sand, means less sand has to be dug out of the ground)

- recycling saves energy (which reduces air pollution).

With older pupils these points could be brought out using a series of questions.

You could then go on to talk about local recycling facilities and any arrangements in school to recycle materials.

End the assembly by reminding pupils that they should not leave litter anywhere; they should always put their rubbish in a bin. But even better than that, where possible they should recycle as many materials as they can, as a way of reducing pollution.

**Related assembly**    Switch it off

**Additional notes**    This assembly is an ideal way to introduce any major school-based litter or recycling campaign. Follow it up with a poster competition.

# Switch it off

**Theme**  Energy conservation, and pollution

**Date**  No specific date

**Materials**  Electric lamp
Two large pieces of paper, each with one of the following sayings written on it:
'Switch the lights off. You're flooding the world'
'Switch the lights off. You're killing the fish.'

**Assembly organization**  Start the assembly by switching on the lamp and asking for two volunteers to hold up the signs, one either side of the light. Explain to the pupils that you want to start that day's assembly by looking at the connection between the light and the two sayings. Go on to ask how most of the electricity in this country is produced. Bring out the answer: By burning coal, oil or gas (fossil fuels).

Next ask the pupils if they can name two gases which are produced as part of the pollution resulting from burning fuels. Bring out the answers: Carbon dioxide and sulphur dioxide. (With younger children, you may need to supply the answers.)

Explain that these two gases are partly responsible for the pollution represented in the two sayings.

Take each saying in turn and explain its connection with the production of electricity. (With older pupils you could bring out this information using a series of questions.)

**Switch the lights off. You're flooding the world**  Some scientists believe that the carbon dioxide produced by burning fossil fuels is contributing to something called the Greenhouse Effect. This is making the Earth warmer and may result in the ice at the North and South Poles melting. This in turn causes sea levels to rise, flooding many areas of low-lying land.

**Switch the lights off. You're killing the fish**  Some scientists believe that the sulphur dioxide produced by burning fossil fuels is dissolving in rain water to produce acid rain. This in turn causes lakes and rivers to become acid and kills the fish. (The information given here has been kept simple for use with younger children; with older ones you can give more detail.)

Go on to explain that the way we produce electricity in this country causes pollution. But we cannot manage without electricity today.

Ask the pupils what things in their house use electricity. Follow this by bringing out a substantial list of appliances that work using electricity. Explain to pupils that many objects, like chairs, don't use electricity but have been manufactured by machinery and in factories which do.

Ask the pupils the question, if we cannot manage without electricity what can we do to reduce this pollution? Bring out the answer: Not waste electricity. By asking questions guide the pupils into suggesting ways of stopping this waste. Examples might be:

- Not switching on lights when they are not needed
- Switching off lights that are not needed. (Switch off the light at the front at this point.)
- Switching off other electrical appliances when they are not needed.
- Wearing extra clothes to keep warm rather than putting on/turning up the heating.
- Having a shower rather than a bath.

Here you could give details about general forms of pollution which are affecting the Earth. Some examples might be:

Car exhausts
Oil spillages
The use of pesticides
Litter

Conclude by saying that the pupils may have to live in the world for another 60 to 70 years so it is important for them to do what they can to keep the world as nice a place as possible to live in. They can help by doing their bit to reduce waste and pollution.

**Related assembly**    Litter

**Additional notes**    If you wished, you could use this assembly to encourage pupils to produce posters promoting energy conservation for display around school.

# It's their world too

**Theme**  Conservation of habitats and species

**Date**  No specific date

**Materials**  Large pictures of animals in danger of becoming extinct (for example, mountain gorilla, cheetah, African elephant, giant panda, whales, rhinoceros, etc.)
Large map of the world

**Assembly organization**  Start the assembly by asking volunteers to hold up the animal pictures and large map of the world in front of the assembly. Ask the pupils what the connection is between these animals. Bring out the answer: They are all in danger of becoming extinct. Go on to talk about each animal you have used, showing the assembly where the animal lives on the world map. Examples of endangered animals might include:

**Mountain gorilla**  Found in Rwanda. Poachers have killed many of the mountain gorillas, reducing their numbers almost to extinction. There are approximately 400 left in the wild. The animals are killed because some people want parts of the gorilla's body as ornaments. (Hands can be used as ash trays.)

**Cheetah**  Found in Africa. The fastest animal on land. The number of cheetahs is currently about 15,000. They are killed for their skins and are in danger of extinction through loss of habitat.

**African elephant**  Found in Africa. Largest land animal. How can you tell an African elephant from an Indian Elephant? Bring out the answer: African elephants have large ears. Poachers in the past have slaughtered up to 100,000 elephants a year. They are killed for their tusks which are used to make ivory ornaments.

**Giant panda**  Found in China. There are believed to be approximately 1000 pandas left in the wild. They are dying out mainly because of loss of habitat.

**Whales**    Found in the oceans of the world. The blue whale is the largest animal ever to live. There are many different species of whale, many of which have been hunted almost to the point of extinction for their meat.

**Rhinoceros**    Found in Africa and Asia. Rhinoceroses are hunted for their horns which are used to make traditional medicines or dagger handles. There are believed to be about 2000 black rhinoceroses left, and only 50 Javan rhinoceroses.

After talking about some specific animals in danger, you might like to move on to some general reasons why so many animals are in danger of becoming extinct. They are:

- hunted for food
- hunted for their skins, tusks, etc.
- poisoned by pollution
- driven out by destruction of their habitat.

Move on to talk about the destruction of tropical rain forests, which are being cut down to provide:

- hardwoods for furniture
- ground to grow food.

Show pupils on the world map where some of the tropical rain forests are located:

- Indonesia
- Brazil
- Central Africa.

You might like to add that at times an area the size of ten football pitches is being cut down every minute, and relate this to the size of the school grounds.

Explain that rain forests provide a habitat for millions of animals and plant species. Some of the plants have already provided useful drugs and foods, and scientists believe that there may be many more still be discovered. So when rain forests are cut down it is not only the lives of many plants and animal species which are put in danger. Supplies of useful foods and drugs are also threatened. Trees take in carbon dioxide and give out oxygen. By cutting down such large numbers of trees we may also be disturbing the balance of gases in the air.

Conclude the assembly by pointing out that we do not have the right to destroy other plant and animal species. Moreover, if we continue to force plants and animals into extinction we run the risk of affecting the quality of our own lives.

**Related assemblies**  None

# Personal qualities

In this group of assemblies you will have the opportunity to bring out a number of different personal qualities. You will find that some of the assemblies provide alternative ways to cover the same topic with different groups of pupils.

| Assembly | Theme |
|---|---|
| Robert Bruce, King of Scotland | *If at first you don't succeed, try, try, again* |
| The road to Damascus | *No one is perfect (changing character)* |
| The seed sower | *The progress you make at school depends on the effort you put in* |
| The Olympic Games | *It's not the winning but the taking part that counts* |
| To be the best | *Always try your hardest* |
| If a job is worth doing | *Do things to the best of your ability* |
| It's only a white lie | *The unacceptability of lying* |
| The tortoise and the hare | *Learn to get on with others* |
| Friends | *The importance of good friends* |
| Rules are there to be broken | *The importance of rules* |
| Don't judge a book by its cover | *Don't judge only by appearances* |
| The wreck of the *Forfarshire* (Grace Darling) | *Equality of opportunity (bravery is not just a male quality)* |
| Finders keepers | *Honesty* |

# Robert Bruce, King of Scotland

**Theme**   If at first you don't succeed, try, try, again

**Date**   No specific date

**Materials**   None

**Assembly organization**   Start the assembly by asking the pupils to complete this famous saying: 'If at first you don't succeed . . .' Explain the meaning of the saying and go on to ask what personal quality this saying illustrates. Bring out the answer: Determination.

Now talk to the pupils about situations in life and in school when determination is needed, for example, when completing a difficult piece of homework. Go on to explain that you are going to tell them a legend about a famous Scottish king.

The man concerned is Robert Bruce who was crowned King of Scotland in 1306, although the English would not accept him as such. He secretly trained an army which defeated the English at the Battle of Bannockburn in 1314. The two countries continued to be at war until 1328 when the English finally recognized Robert Bruce as King of Scotland. Robert Bruce died one year after this in 1329.

The legend says that, after his coronation in 1306, Robert Bruce was forced to hide as a fugitive. Once, while hiding in a cottage and feeling discouraged (ready to give up), the King watched a spider trying to build its web from one beam to another. Six times the spider tried and six times it failed. Robert Bruce said to himself, 'If it tries again and succeeds, I will make another attempt to regain my throne.' At the seventh try, the spider succeeded. Likewise, Robert Bruce defeated the English and retained his crown. The legend is probably not true but it is true that Robert Bruce needed great determination to retain his crown.

Round off the story by pointing out that pupils will never be faced with a situation as serious as the one Robert Bruce was in, but that in everyday life there are many occasions when determination is needed. Without it they will never finish a difficult job.

Give further examples of where determination in life and school is needed.

Finally, end by reminding the pupils of the saying with which you started the assembly: 'If at first you don't succeed, try, try, again.'

**Related assemblies**    None

# The road to Damascus

**Theme**   No one is perfect (changing character)

**Date**   In the week of 25 January (St Paul's Day)

**Materials**   None

**Assembly organization**   Start the assembly by asking the pupils what it means to be perfect. Bring out the answer: To behave in a sensible way, not to be naughty, to have no faults and do nothing wrong, etc. Ask the pupils if they have heard people use the saying: 'No one is perfect.' Explain that this means that all people do things wrong sometimes, and that everyone has something they could change or improve.

Go on to explain that the first part of making any changes in their behaviour or character is to realize and admit that they have a fault that needs to be improved or changed. (Stress, of course, that you are talking about changes for the better. The idea is to see people improving themselves, not changing from good to bad.)

Next point out that people do not always realize their own faults and sometimes, as a friend, it may be necessary to point out someone's weaknesses. This should be done tactfully of course. Contrast two possible ways of saying the same thing. For example:

'You're always so miserable, you are.'

'You don't seem to be very happy now-a-days.'

Ask pupils which is the best way to point out a friend's weakness.

Having realized the need for a change in character, the next step is to make the necessary efforts to bring about that change. Explain that you want to tell them about something that happened nearly 2000 years ago. Tell them it is a story about a man who made a very dramatic change to his life.

This man disagreed with the beliefs of another group of people at the time. In fact he disagreed with their beliefs so much that he persecuted them. Ask pupils what the word 'persecute' means. Bring out the answer: To harass (get at) someone continually. He went so far with his attack on these people that he asked if he could travel to another city to arrest the people he disagreed with who lived there. The city was Damascus and his change of character took place on the road to Damascus.

As he was on his way the man was struck down by a light which blinded him. What happened to him then and when he reached Damascus totally changed his views and his way of behaving (his character).

When he reached Damascus, he was visited by a man who restored his sight. This man believed in the things the first man had come to persecute. These events changed the first man's attitude and he joined the people he had been persecuting.

Go on to discuss the dramatic nature of the change to the man in the story; if someone can change this much everyone can make the little changes they need to, with a bit of effort. Remind pupils of the two stages of changing character:

- Realizing the weakness or fault that needs to be changed
- Making the necessary effort to bring about the required change.

(Again mention that it is only worth changing for the better.) Say that each person should look at their own weaknesses and try to make the necessary efforts to change them.

In conclusion you could tell the pupils the origin of your story: St Paul's conversion on the road to Damascus and place it in its original context. (See *Acts 9, 1–25*) Finally, point out that 25 January is St Paul's Day.

**Related assemblies**     None

# The seed sower

**Theme**   The progress you make at school depends on the effort you put in

**Date**   During early spring

**Materials**   Packets of seeds

**Assembly organization**   Start the assembly by talking about planting seeds in a garden, about how they grow and develop if they get a good start. Explain that, in some ways, the pupils' development in school is like the growth of seeds; they represent the seeds, and the school and their lessons represent the soil. If they get a good start they should be able to achieve their full potential.

Go on to explain what you mean by this, using the following examples:

***Some seeds fall amongst weeds***   These seeds grow well to begin with but slow down when the weeds grow up and choke them. This is like those pupils who fall in with the wrong sort of friends. They are encouraged to waste time and to do wrong things. Having made a reasonable start these pupils fail to make a success of their time at school.

***Some seeds fall on hard, bare ground***   These seeds never started growing. There was no way their roots could get into the soil. This is like those pupils who come to school but do not do their work, do not do their homework, waste time and are generally lazy. These pupils do not improve because they do not try and they leave school having made little progress.

***Some seeds fall into good soil***   These seeds grow well and soon develop into strong, healthy plants. This is like those pupils who come to school and always try their best and get on with their work. These pupils improve year after year and go on to make a success of their time in school.

At this stage you might also like to introduce the saying, 'You can take a horse to water, but you cannot make it drink'. Again explain how this can be likened to their time in school. They have to come to school and they can be made to behave; they can be made to get on with their work but only they can decide to do their absolute best. Go on to explain that, like the seeds, they all have the potential to develop well. In school they have what they need to do their very best and to make a success of their education. However, they must take the opportunity and not waste time or be distracted by friends.

You might like to conclude by asking the pupils if they can tell you where the original story of the seed sower came from. Go on to explain the meaning of the original parable told by Jesus in *Matthew's Gospel, chapter 13, 1–9*.

**Related assemblies**　None

# The Olympic Games

**Theme**   It's not the winning but the taking part that counts

**Date**   Any time during an Olympic year

**Materials**   Large pieces of paper with the following cities and years written on. (NB The list needs to be updated every four years.)

|  |  |
|------|------|
| Rome | 1960 |
| Tokyo | 1964 |
| Mexico City | 1968 |
| Munich | 1972 |
| Montreal | 1976 |
| Moscow | 1980 |
| Los Angeles | 1984 |
| Seoul | 1988 |
| Barcelona | 1992 |

Large replica on white paper of the Olympic five-ring flag. (This contains the colours: blue, yellow, black, green and red, in that order.)

**Assembly organization**   From the assembly as a whole, or from your own form, collect eighteen volunteers. (The number of pupils can be reduced if you wish by only using the more recent dates and venues.) Give each pupil one of the dates or cities listed above, put them in a line and ask them to show their piece of paper. (Make certain that the cities and dates are not given out in the correct order.) Ask the assembly if they can see a connection between the cities and the dates.

Ask if anyone can match up the dates and the cities; this can be done by matching them one by one, starting with the most recent venue: Barcelona 1992. (An alternative would be to ask a member of staff to arrange all the cities and dates in the correct order.)

Next go on to explain a little of the history of the Olympic Games.

The Olympic Games first started as athletic sporting events organized by the Ancient Greeks more than two thousand years ago. They were part of a festival held in honour of the Greek god, Zeus. The modern

Olympics were started in Athens in 1896 by a Frenchman, Baron Pierre de Coubertin.

Show the pupils the replica Olympic flag. Explain that the five different coloured rings represent the five continents. The six colours used (the five rings and white background) are present in the flags of all the countries of the world. The motto: *Citius, Altius, Fortius* was adopted in 1922. It means: Swifter, Higher, Stronger. However, there is another saying more widely connected with the Olympic Games. It was part of a speech made by Baron Pierre de Coubertin and is: 'The most important thing in the Olympic Games is not to win but to take part.'

At this point you might like to express the opinion that this original motto has been lost in modern Olympics. Many top competitors do not compete just for the honour of taking part. They can receive large amounts of money from sponsorship deals if they are successful in the Olympic Games.

Conclude by pointing out that the motto 'it's not the winning, but the taking part' is an important idea which should not be forgotten. It is true in all sporting events, where it is important to enjoy the activity whether you win or lose. It is also true in other areas of life, including lessons at school, where it is important for everyone to take part, to try their best and always to enjoy what they are doing.

You might like to end by referring back to Baron Pierre de Coubertin's original speech in which he also made this point:

'The important thing in the Olympic Games is not to win but to take part, just as the important thing in life is not the triumph but the struggle.'

Then stress the point that in all areas of life the important thing is to try your best, to enjoy yourself and be pleased with your achievements.

**Related assemblies**    To be the best
If a job's worth doing

# To be the best

**Theme** Always trying your hardest

**Date** No specific date

**Materials** None

**Assembly organization** Read out to the pupils, one by one, a list of famous people, sports stars, actors/actresses, singers, scientists, designers, etc. (Choose ones the pupils will know.) After each name ask the pupils how they know of that person, and what he or she does. (Don't use the word 'famous'.) Next ask: What do they all have in common? Bring out the answer: They are all famous.

Go on to talk about the fact that the people mentioned have reached the top of their chosen career; they are all the best at what they do. Move on to explain that not everyone can become the best at what they do and that most people have to be happy with being second or third best.

Choose one or two examples of sports stars who are well known for achievements through hard training and fair play. They should be individuals who might be known by the pupils, as they are intended as good role models whose values the pupils can take on – even if they do not achieve the same standard of achievement. Examples might be:

- Gary Lineker – who was never booked in all the years he played football.

- Linford Christie – who was proud that he achieved his Olympic 100m gold medal without cheating (without using drugs).

- Sally Gunnell – who won Olympic and World Championship Gold medals and says that the one thing she always keeps in mind is the importance of enjoying each event, whether or not she wins.

If you use these examples you might like to tell the pupils each name and then ask them a few questions about that person's sport and achievements.

Talk about your chosen stars and explain how they have tried their hardest to do well and have become famous by doing their best and not by cheating or being unfair.

Conclude by talking about the fact that being the best at something isn't what matters; we cannot all become famous for being the best. What really matters is knowing that however well you do, you have tried your best and done as well as you can.

Finally, say that in school they cannot all be the best in class and cannot be brilliant at everything. What matters is that they have all tried their best and know that whatever they do achieve, it is the best they can do. If they have tried their best they can be proud of their achievements, and so can their parents. No one can expect them to do more.

**Related assemblies**  The Olympic Games
If a job is worth doing

# If a job is worth doing

**Theme**  Do things to the best of your ability

**Date**  No specific date

**Materials**  Eleven large pieces of paper. On each piece write one word from the following saying: 'If a job is worth doing, it is worth doing well.'
Child's wooden building bricks

**Assembly organization**  **S**tart the assembly by asking for eleven volunteers and giving each one a piece of paper from your saying to hold up. Ask the pupils what they think this saying means. Bring out the answer: You should always do things to the best of your ability. Next go on to explain to the pupils that you want them to listen to a story which illustrates this point. Tell them the following story:

Many years ago a man employed a young builder to build a house. This particular builder was given the job as he was soon to marry one of the man's servants. They agreed on a price and the man explained that he was going away on a journey and wanted the house built for when he returned. The builder was glad his employer was going away as he knew many dishonest ways to help him make more money. He would:

- use thin beams under the floor where they couldn't be seen. These would break if anything heavy was placed on them
- make the doors and windows of unseasoned wood, which would swell in damp weather and not open
- take no care putting in the drains; they would easily block
- fill the cracks between the woodwork with filler, then paint over it.

When his employer returned, the builder said what a wonderful house he had built and that not a better one was to be found for miles around. His employer said he was pleased that the young man was so happy with the house as . . .

Ask the pupils what they think the employer said next. Bring out the answer: He was giving the house to the young man as his wedding present. Ask the pupils how they think the builder felt when he heard this. Then ask what they think the builder wished he had done when he heard this? Bring out the answer: Made a good job of building the house.

Conclude the assembly by explaining that every day at school, pupils are building their future. You could relate this to building a house and relate each year to a layer of bricks; if the layers are not built well, the house will fall down. (You could demonstrate this by building a tower with the wooden bricks.)

Finally, remind the pupils that they should not be like the builder in the story; they should always do their best to give themselves a chance of the best possible future.

**Related assemblies**   The Olympic Games
To be the best

# It's only a white lie

**Theme**  The unacceptability of lying

**Date**  No specific date

**Materials**  None

**Assembly organization**  Before the assembly, collect a number of volunteers from your form to act out the following scenes:

1  A pupil is caught by a teacher with a pen which is not hers.
2  A mother has cooked a special meal for her daughter's birthday but the daughter does not like it.
3  Parents have found a broken ornament at home and ask their son what happened.
4  A boy has just bought some new clothes (which don't suit him) and asks his best friend what he thinks of them.

You will need to make provision for each group of pupils to practise their mini-play.

In situations **1** and **3** the individual needs to lie and try to blame someone else to protect themselves. In situations **2** and **4** the individual needs to tell lies to protect the feelings of the other person who feels all is not well.

Make it clear to the pupils that the assembly is going to look at lies. Say that you want them to watch four short plays. Ask the volunteers to perform their plays.

Once the four plays have been performed say to pupils that each play showed someone telling lies. Explain that they can be divided into two different types. Ask the pupils to tell you how the situations are different. Bring out the answer: Two situations are lies to protect yourself and two are lies to protect someone else's feelings (white lies).

Go on to divide the situations into lies and white lies. Talk about how white lies can sometimes seem to protect someone else's feelings, but that lies are actually an attempt to get yourself out of trouble. They usually make matters worse by getting you into more trouble.

Next say to the pupils that you want to take a look at the white lies in a little more detail. Bring out the following points:

**Situation 2**  If you tell your mother that the meal is nice, she may cook it again and you will have to keep lying about it. She could cook it for someone else and they may tell her it isn't very good, which would hurt her feelings even more.

**Situation 4**  If you tell your friend the clothes look nice then they will go around wearing them and other people will think the same as you. Someone will eventually tell your friend that the clothes don't suit them and that will hurt their feelings.

Conclude by pointing out that it is always best to tell the truth. Telling lies to get yourself out of trouble or to protect someone's feelings only makes matters worse and gets you into more trouble.

Finally, relate this to the saying, 'honesty is the best policy'.

**Related assemblies**  None

# The tortoise and the hare

**Theme** Learn to get on with others

**Date** No specific date

**Materials** Additional notes (see page 73): summary of 'The tortoise and the hare'

**Assembly organization** You can tell the story of the tortoise and the hare as given in the Additional notes, or you can organize a group of volunteers to act out the story.

Start the assembly by saying that today you want to look at two aspects of school life. (With younger pupils you might use the word 'sides' instead of aspects.) The first aspect is learning about all the subjects the pupils cover. The second aspect is how the pupils get on with other people and the sort of person they are. Say that you want to start by looking at a story they will all have heard.

Tell the story of 'The tortoise and the hare', (or ask your volunteers to act it out).

Ask the pupils if they can tell you the name of the story. Bring out the answer: The story of 'The tortoise and the hare' which is one of Aesop's Fables. Go on to ask about the personality of the tortoise and the hare. Bring out these points:

The hare is a big-head, a show-off.
The tortoise is quiet, modest.

Ask the pupils which character they would rather have as a friend. Bring out the answer: The tortoise. Go on to bring out reasons why the hare wouldn't be a nice friend:

He's too big headed.
He's nasty to his friends (the tortoise)
He's a show-off.

Next go on to talk about how certain types of people aren't liked; their personalities make them unpopular.

Ask the pupils to give some examples of types of people they would not like as friends. Some answers to bring out might be:

| big heads | unkind people |
| show-offs | bullies |

Next go on to talk about how there are certain types of people who make good friends. Some answers to bring out might be:

polite   reliable
helpful   kind

Conclude that these are the qualities that you want in a good friend, and the sort of quality teachers hope to help pupils develop at school.

Finally, ask the pupils who won the race between the tortoise and the hare. Mention that there is another thing about being big-headed; the person often comes unstuck and ends up looking rather foolish.

**Related assembly**  Friends

**Additional notes**

*Summary of 'The tortoise and the hare'*  In telling the story, portray the hare as a big-headed and arrogant character.

When the tortoise and the hare met one day, the hare made fun of the tortoise's slow life-style because he could not run as fast as the hare. After a while, when the tortoise had enough of the hare making fun of him, he challenged the hare to a race.

While the hare continued to make fun of the tortoise, the tortoise started the race. Once the hare realized what had happened he ran off and overtook the tortoise.

When the hare was near to the finish line, he lay down and took a rest, but he fell asleep. While the hare was sleeping the tortoise overtook the sleeping hare to cross the winning line first and to win the race.

# Friends

**Theme**   The importance of good friends

**Date**   No specific date

**Materials**   None

**Assembly organization**   Ask the pupils to complete this saying: 'A friend in need, . . .'. Talk to them about the saying and bring out that a friend who only bothers with you when they have a problem is not really a good friend.

Change the saying to: 'A friend who helps you when you are in need, is a friend indeed.' Go on to explain that someone who is prepared to help you when you have a problem is a good friend. Say that you want to spend the rest of the assembly looking at qualities pupils should look for in good friends.

Some points you might like to bring out are that good friends:

- do not call you names behind your back
- like some of the things you do
- can disagree with you without arguing
- do not bully you
- would not try to make you do something you do not want to (e.g. smoking)
- are prepared to help you if you have a problem
- do not gossip about you behind your back
- do not bribe you for your friendship
- do not steal things from you.

These points and others can be brought out straight away by asking the pupils what they expect of a good friend. Or you could ask pointed questions, such as:

If someone gives you sweets to be their friend, would you call them a good friend? (Some of these points could also be organized as small group mini-plays.)

You might like to refer the pupils to the following ideas of friendship from the Bible:

- Do not make friends with people who have a violent

temper as you might develop a violent temper yourself. (*Proverbs 22, 24–5*)

● Do not try to make friends with unpleasant people as all they can do is cause trouble and hurt people. (*Proverbs 24, 1–2*)

Conclude the assembly by pointing out that everyone needs good friends and that life without friends can be very lonely. It is important to be sure that your friends are good; they don't bully you and they don't get you into trouble.

　　　　　Finally, point out that one way to help make sure your friends are good ones is to be a good friend yourself.

**Related assembly**　The tortoise and the hare

# Rules are there to be broken

**Theme** The importance of rules

**Date** This assembly can be useful during the first few weeks with a new intake year group

**Materials** None

**Assembly organization**

**S**tart the assembly by introducing the saying 'Rules are there to be broken'. Talk about what life would be like if rules really were there to be broken, or if we had no rules.

Discuss with the pupils the rules necessary to play any game you are familiar with.

- What rules are there?
- Why are they there?
- What would the game be like without them?

Move on from sport to talk about the Highway Code.

- What is it?
- Why is it against the law to cycle on the path?

Conclude by pointing out that the Highway Code is there to protect people.

Ask the pupils if they know of any other rules that are there to protect people. Examples might be:

- you are not allowed to play on railway lines
- it is against the law to kill someone.

Talk to the pupils about rules not being there to be broken but to protect people.

Ask if anyone can think of another reason why we have rules. Bring out the answer: To protect property.

Now move on to talk about the school's rules and why there are rules in school. Ask pupils if the rules are there to protect people or property. Some examples could be:

- do not run around school
- do not write on the walls.

You could conclude by talking to the pupils about the

very important set of rules that apply to the way Christians and Jews live their lives: the Ten Commandments. (If time allows you could explain a little about how they were given to Moses.) Talk about some of the Commandments, for example:

- Do not kill
- Do not steal.

Explain how they are part of the rules for everyday life. (See *Exodus 20, 1–17*)

**Related assemblies**    None

# Don't judge a book by its cover

**Theme**   Don't judge only by appearances

**Date**   No specific date

**Materials**   None

**Assembly organization**

**B**efore the assembly, ask for six volunteers from your form to take the following parts:

two thieves          one police officer
one victim           one football supporter
one priest

You will need to find time for them to rehearse their parts in this mini-play.

Start the assembly by asking the pupils if they have heard the saying: 'Don't judge a book by its cover'. Explain the meaning of the saying and point out that this applies to all sorts of things. People should not make judgements without finding out more information to help them decide. Go on to explain that you want to look at a story which illustrates this point.

Ask the volunteers to act out the story of the Good Samaritan, and explain the story as it develops.

**Narrator**   Here we see a man out for a walk in the countryside. He is set upon by two thieves who beat him up and rob him. After taking his wallet the thieves leave him for dead.

○ *Two thieves mime attacking the man and robbing him. Once they have taken his money the thieves run off, leaving the man on the floor.*

**Narrator**   The man was left on the ground, unable to help himself. Along came a priest who was also out for a stroll in the countryside. When he saw the man he was concerned but felt he himself might be set upon. So he crossed the road and walked by.

○ *Priest mimes strolling in the country looking around. He mimes concern when he sees the body but moves away from the man and walks past.*

**Narrator**   Next came along an off-duty police officer out for a walk.

She too saw the body and was concerned, but she knew if she helped she would have to spend the day at the police station filling in paperwork. So she crossed the road and walked by.

○ *Police officer mimes walking in the country looking around. She mimes concern when she sees the body, but moves away from the man and walks past.*

**Narrator**   Finally, along came a football supporter.

Ask pupils what sort of reputation football supporters have and what they expect might happen. Bring out the answer: Some of them are hooligans and would walk past the man or try to take things from him.

**Narrator**   When he saw the man the football supporter went over, gave him a drink, helped him up and took him to a local hospital.

○ *Football supporter mimes walking along in the country looking around. He mimes concern when he sees the body and then goes over and helps the man to stand up.*

Point out to the pupils that this story illustrates that you cannot make judgements about people based merely on their appearance. You need to find out more about them before deciding.

Conclude by asking the pupils if they know which story this play was based on. Tell them it is a story told by Jesus from the Christian Bible. (See *Luke 10, 25–37*). You might then finish off by going over the story of the Good Samaritan to reinforce the point.

**Related assembly**   The wreck of the *Forfarshire*

# The wreck of the *Forfarshire* (Grace Darling)

**Theme**    Equality of opportunity (bravery is not just a male quality)

**Date**    In the week of 7 September (date the rescue took place)

**Materials**    None

**Assembly organization**    You will need to find time for the pupils to rehearse the mini-play before the assembly. Choose four pupils to take the parts:

> two crew members
> one young girl
> Grace's father.

Explain to the pupils in the assembly that you are going to talk to them about a true story and that at the end you would like them to tell you who it is about.

**Narrator**    Here we see the crew of a ship sailing along nearly 150 years ago. They are sailing around the Farne Islands, just off the coast of Northumberland.
○ *Two crew members mime hoisting the sails and steering ship.*

**Narrator**    Later that evening, the ship was hit by a terrible storm.
○ *Crew mime being shaken about on the boat, by the storm.*

**Narrator**    The next day a father and his daughter were out walking when they saw the crew clinging to the wrecked ship.
○ *Crew mime clinging to the ship and waving for help. Girl with father mime walking and spotting the wrecked ship and crew.*

**Narrator**    The young girl urged her father that they should take out a boat and row over to the ship to rescue the survivors.
○ *The girl pulls at her father's arm and pleads with him.*

**Narrator**    The storm was still raging but nevertheless the young girl and her father rowed their boat out to the wreck.
○ *The girl and her father mime rowing their boat.*

**Narrator**   That day the young girl and her father rescued five
people from the wrecked ship.
  O *The young girl and her father mime collecting the survivors
and rowing back to safety.*

Ask the pupils if they know the name of the girl in this
story. (If they do not know the answer, ask the staff if
they can say who it is.) The story illustrates the heroism
of a young girl called Grace Darling who insisted on
rowing out with her father to the wreck of the *Forfarshire*
and rescuing five people.

The actions of Grace and her father soon
became famous and they were later awarded gold medals
by the Humane Society. Ask the pupils which quality
Grace Darling showed. Bring out the answer: Bravery.
Explain that in those days bravery was thought to be a
quality which only men had; women were not expected
to show bravery. Today we know better not to judge
what personal qualities an individual may have just by
their appearance.

Ask the pupils if they can name any careers
requiring bravery that women and men can take up
today. Bring out the answers: Police officer, Fire officer,
Armed services (Army, Navy, Air force).

If you wish you can relate the idea of not
judging a person by their appearance to the story of the
Good Samaritan. At the time of the story of the Good
Samaritan the Samaritan would have been considered the
least likely of the three travellers to stop and help the
injured man. (See *Luke 10, 25–37*)

Conclude by pointing out that the wreck of the
*Forfarshire* was an unavoidable accident that happened
because of a terrible storm. Ask the pupils what
organization they would hope to see coming to their
rescue if they ever got into difficulty by the sea. Bring out
the answer: The RNLI (The Royal National Lifeboat
Institution).

**Related
assembly**   Don't judge a book by its cover

# Finders keepers

**Theme** Honesty

**Date** No specific date

**Materials** Four large pieces of paper, each with one word of the following saying, written on it:
'Finders keepers, loser weepers'

**Assembly organization** Before the assembly you will need to arrange for a group of four pupils to practise a mini-play. Two of the pupils are walking and talking, and one of them drops a wallet and walks on. These two are followed by two other pupils. One finds the wallet and wants to keep it, the other suggests it should be handed in.

Start the assembly by asking four volunteers to come to the front and hold up the four words. (Ensure the words are not in the correct order.) Ask the pupils if they can rearrange these words to make a famous saying. Using the pupils' suggestions rearrange the four volunteers to make the saying. Ask what this saying means. Bring out the answer: People who lose things will be upset and sad, while those who find something will keep it and be happy.

Ask the four pupils to act out their mini play. At the end ask the assembly how they think the play ends. Some answers to bring out might be:

1 They get away with keeping the wallet. (This is not fair to the person who lost the wallet.)
2 They are seen picking up the wallet. (This gets them into trouble with the police as people said they stole it.)
3 They chase after the people and return the wallet. (This makes the person who dropped the wallet happy and he/she gives them a reward.)
4 They take the wallet into the police station. (They did not see who dropped the wallet so they took it into the police station. After about six weeks, if no one claims the wallet, the police will give it back to them as a reward for handing it in.)

Ask the pupils which of these endings shows the best thing to do. Bring out the answer: Either **3** or **4**, depending whether they saw who dropped the wallet. They do not end up in trouble and they have done the right thing.

(You may like to explain the origins of the Ten Commandments before this final section of the assembly.)

Explain to the pupils that situations like the one in the play, when people are tempted to take what is not theirs (stealing things), is covered by the eighth Commandment. Ask the pupils what they think the eighth Commandment says. Bring out the answer: You should not steal.

You might like at this point to spend some time talking about the other nine Commandments. (See *Exodus 20, 1–17*.)

Conclude by reminding the pupils that 'Honesty is always the best policy' and that they should never steal anything.

**Related assemblies** None

# Money and the consumer society

These assemblies are intended to provide you with the opportunity to cover topics relating to greed and the pressures of today's consumer society.

| Assembly | Theme |
| --- | --- |
| The boss's new clothes | *Fashion, peer group and advertising pressure* |
| Seeing is believing | *Consumer advertising pressure* |
| Probably so | *You do not get something for nothing* |
| Decision making | *Important decisions through life and ways of making them* |
| The love of money is the root of all evil | *The unacceptability of greed* |

# The boss's new clothes

**Theme**  Fashion, peer group and advertising pressure

**Date**  No specific date

**Materials**  Items of extreme fashion

**Assembly organization**  Arrange for a group of eight pupils from your form to act out the following mini-play. (You will need to provide time for the pupils to rehearse their actions.)

Explain to the assembly that you want them to watch this short play and then tell you which story it is based upon.

**Narrator**  Here we see the owner of a large factory talking with a travelling designer about some new clothes he would like.

O  *Boss, sitting down, looking at the materials being shown to him by the designer.*

**Narrator**  Now the designer tries to convince the boss to buy some new material and have his clothes made from it.

O  *Designer mimes showing the boss some new material. The boss should look at the material very quizzically.*

**Narrator**  What the boss does not realize is that the designer is trying to swindle him. The material does not really exist, but the designer tells him only fools cannot see the cloth. She hopes to persuade the boss to pay money for something which will cost nothing to make. The boss agrees to have his clothes made from this wonderful new material.

O  *Boss mimes looking pleased with the material and agreeing to have his new clothes made up with it.*

**Narrator**  Here we see the designer coming back with the clothes that have been made from the invisible material. The boss tries on his new clothes and is very pleased with them. He pays the designer.

O  *Boss looks pleased with the new clothes the designer mimes holding up.*
*The boss mimes trying on his new clothes and models them*

*looking very pleased.*
*The boss mimes paying for his new clothes.*

**Narrator**  Now we see the boss modelling his new clothes for some of his employees. Notice the confused looks on their faces; they have heard that only fools cannot see the cloth.

O *Boss walks over to where the group of employees are seated, and mimes modelling his new clothes for them.*

**Narrator**  None of the employees wants to seem a fool nor do they want to upset the boss, so they all decide to tell him how nice his new clothes are.

O *Employees all pass comment on the clothes, such as:* 'smart', 'cool', 'trendy', *etc.*

**Narrator**  Finally, as the boss walks away looking pleased with himself, a visitor to the factory walks past him towards the group of employees and says: 'Does your boss always walk around with nothing on?'

Ask the pupils which story this mini play is based on. Bring out the answer: The emperor's new clothes. Ask if they think they would ever fall for a trick like that one.
    Go on to show the pupils the items of extreme fashion you have collected, e.g. large kipper ties, platform shoes, flared trousers with coloured inserts, and talk about how silly or impractical they are. (If you do not have examples of these items you could describe them instead.)
    Ask the pupils if they think these items look good. Ask how many of them would like to wear them. What do they think made people buy them? Bring out the following reasons:

• pressure from their friends to wear this type of clothing

• advertising pressure – these were *the* clothes to wear.

Next bring the conversation round to talk about whatever the extreme fashion of the day might be. Suggest that, just as they would not dream of buying the items you have shown them, today's fashion will seem equally ridiculous in a few years' time.
    Conclude by pointing out that advertising and pressure from their friends can make them buy

something that normally they would not dream of purchasing. They should always choose things that they see as reasonable and that they like, not just what is fashionable at that moment, otherwise they may be stuck with something they will never want to wear again. (You could also draw the pupils' attention to the high cost of fashion items.)

**Related assembly**     Seeing is believing

# Seeing is believing

**Theme**     Consumer advertising pressure

**Date**     No specific date

**Materials**     OHPs 1–3: Optical illusions (pages 90–2)
Overhead projector and screen

**Assembly organization**     **S**tart the assembly by asking the pupils if they have heard of the saying: 'Seeing is believing'. Talk about the meaning of this saying. Go on to explain that you want to examine this saying to find out if it is true that you can believe what you see.

Show the pupils OHP 1. Ask them which line seems the longest. Bring out the answer: B. Then go on to measure both lines and show that they are the same length.

Show the pupils OHP 2. Ask them what they can see. Bring out the two answers: A goblet, and Two people nose to nose.

Show the pupils OHP 3. Ask them what they notice about the two lines across the middle. Bring out the answer: They are curved. Then go on to measure the distance between the lines and show that they are actually straight lines.

Next point out that from these three simple illusions it can be seen that you cannot always believe what you see. Some things are not always what they seem to be.

Next tell the pupils that today you want to concentrate on advertising. You might like to express the opinion that there are two aims behind certain types of advertising. These are:

● to inform people about a product

● to convince people to buy a product.

Tell the pupils that you want to focus on this second aim. Present the idea that one of the jobs of the advert is to use the notion of 'seeing is believing'; advertisers provide an image to believe in and, therefore, a reason to buy their product.

With this idea in mind, some advertising styles to discuss could be:

1 The use of sporting stars to advertise sports related products, which implies:

- they are good at their sport because they use that product
- by using that product you could become as good as they are.

Ask the pupils to name some products that use this approach.

2 The use of luxury homes and expensive cars to advertise various products, which implies:

- the people you see in the advert use these products
- by using these products you could live in the style you see in the advert.

Again, you could ask the pupils to name some products that use this approach.

Next go on to say that there are other devices used in adverts which aim to persuade you to buy the product. Some examples to discuss might me:

1 sponsorship
2 the use of catchy tunes
3 competitions
4 free gifts.

For each advertising device you choose to discuss, illustrate your comments by referring to a current product which uses that advertising style.

Conclude the assembly by reminding the pupils that the purpose of adverts is to inform them about a product, and to persuade them to buy it. Emphasize your starting point: you cannot always believe all that you see. Advise them to use their own thoughts when deciding whether to buy the product and not to be persuaded by what they see in the advert.

**Related assemblies**    The boss's new clothes

# OHP 1

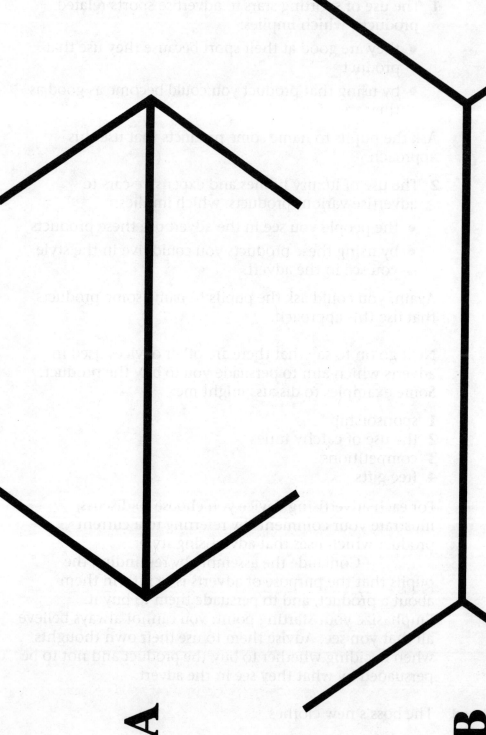

A

B

## OHP 2

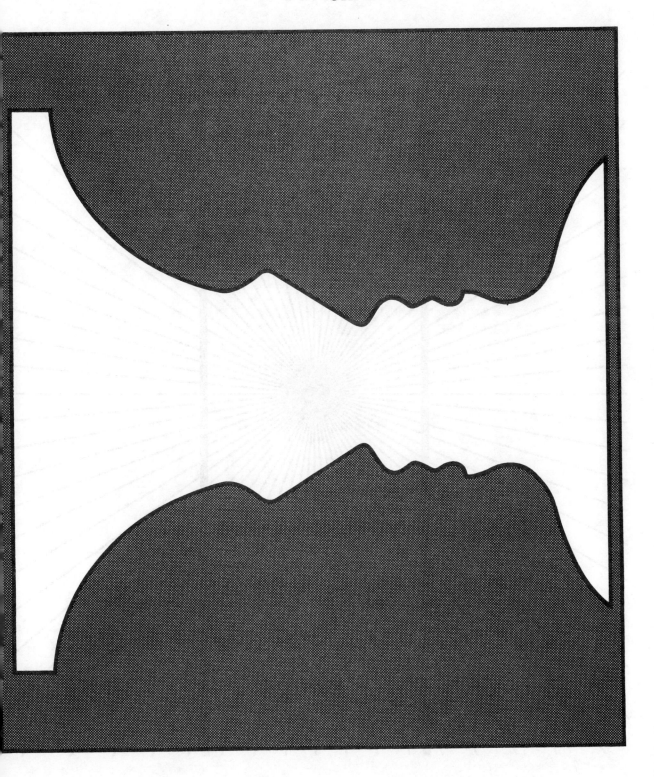

# OHP 3

# Probably so

**Theme**    You do not get something for nothing

**Date**    No specific date

**Materials**    Examples of magazine competitions
Piece of paper with an X on it
Box of 1000 envelopes
OHP: What makes a number one record? (Use page 95 to make the OHP transparency)
Overhead projector and screen
Four answer sheets: What makes a number one record? (Copied from page 95)
One answer sheet filled in

**Assembly organization**    Ask the pupils how many of them have entered a magazine competition recently. Get those who put their hands up to talk about the competitions they have entered:

- What did they have to do?
- What might they have won?
- Did they win?

Next explain to the pupils that many companies use entries to competitions as a way of getting people to buy their product. Look at some of the competitions you have brought in; talk about how you enter and how you win. Ask the pupils if they have heard of the saying: 'You do not get something for nothing'. Point out that most competitions are based on the assumption that most people wish to do just this – to get a major prize by purchasing a small cheap item. Say that next you want to look at what the chances are of winning some competitions. Hold up the chocolate bar and ask the pupils who would like to win it. Pick a number of volunteers from those who put up their hands.

Show all the pupils the piece of paper with the X on it. Place it inside one of the envelopes and place this envelope back in the box. (Do this with the envelope flap facing the opposite direction to the rest of the envelopes; this will allow you to find and remove the piece of paper at the end of the assembly.) Do not allow the volunteers to see where in the box you have placed the winning envelope. Allow each pupil to pick an envelope and see if they have won. Return the envelopes each time.

Ask the pupils what chance they have of winning this competition. Bring out the answer: 1 in a 1000 (1 winning envelope in a box of 1000). Explain that this competition relies purely on luck and that next you want to look at one that relies upon skill.

Put up the OHP: What makes a number 1 record? Ask the pupils if there are any volunteers who think they could put the items in the correct order to produce a hit record. Anyone who gets the answer correct can have the bar of chocolate.

Pick four volunteers and give them a 'What makes a number 1 record?' answer sheet. Explain that all they have to do is to put the items in the correct order. Give them a few minutes to do this.

Meanwhile, talk to the rest of the pupils about the chances of getting the ten statements in the correct order. For them to get all ten statements correct, they have something like a 1 in 3½ million chance.

Collect in the four sheets and compare the order of their answers with the order you decided on earlier. Give the chocolate bar to whoever comes nearest.

Talk to the pupils about how easy it *seems* to put ten statements in the correct order. Look at the number of statements your volunteers had in the correct order and remind pupils that there was only a 1 in 3½ million chance of getting the final order correct.

Conclude by pointing out that you are not trying to stop them entering competitions, but that you want them to look carefully at any competition they do enter. They should try to make sure they are not cheated into buying something when they have little or no chance of winning the competition. (Is the competition fair?) Remind them of the saying from the start of the assembly: 'You do not get something for nothing'.

**Related assemblies**   None

# What makes a number one record?

Place the statements in order of importance, using the boxes provided.

☐ A CATCHY TUNE

☐ MADE BY A WELL-KNOWN GROUP OR SOLO ARTIST

☐ YOU CAN DANCE TO IT

☐ DIFFERENT FROM ALL OTHER RECORDS

☐ LASTS FOR MORE THAN FOUR MINUTES

☐ HAS A CHORUS TO SING ALONG WITH

☐ PLAYED ON RADIO 1

☐ THE RECORD SLEEVE IS ATTRACTIVE

☐ IT HAS A GOOD B-SIDE

☐ THE MESSAGE IN THE SONG

# Decision making

**Theme**  Important decisions through life and ways of making them

**Date**  No specific date

**Materials**  Pack of cards
Three envelopes: one containing a blank piece of paper; two containing pieces of paper stating a punishment (e.g. 100 lines)
Two wrapped presents: apple core wrapped neatly; chocolate bar wrapped in torn old newspaper.
Chocolate bars to give as prizes

**Assembly organization**  Talk to the pupils about how there are many ways of deciding things. Either ask them to give you some examples or go through the list below with them.

- random choice
- guesswork
(mention that these are similar and are both a gamble)
- impulsive choice
- influenced choice
- informed choice

Now go back to each example and bring out the following points:

**Random choice**  In this method you can usually use something over which you have no control to help you make a decision. The result will be purely chance or random; for example after flipping a coin.
  Hold up a chocolate bar and ask who would like a chance of having it. Pick a volunteer. Hold up the pack of cards, ask the volunteer to name a card. Explain that if they pick that card they get the chocolate bar; if not they get a punishment.

**Guesswork**  In this method you must make a guess without giving it any thought.
  Again hold up the chocolate bar and ask who would like a chance of winning it. Pick a volunteer. Hold

up three envelopes – A, B and C – and explain that two contain a punishment and one a blank piece of paper. The blank piece of paper will win the chocolate bar. Ask the volunteer to pick an envelope.

***Impulsive choice***

An impulsive choice is one made on the spur of the moment, with little thought or information. You have no particular reason for buying what you did.

***Influenced choice***

In this case your choice is influenced by something or someone.

Ask for a volunteer. Show the volunteer the two presents; ask them to choose one. Influence their choice by pointing out which looks the best, which looks the nicest, how scruffy one looks. Make sure they choose the nicely wrapped apple core. Let them unwrap their present.

Ask the pupils which method of choosing is left.

***Informed choice***

Point out how any important decision should be an informed one.

Ask for a volunteer. Show the volunteer the three envelopes – A, B and C. Remind him/her that two contain a punishment and one contains a blank piece of paper. Explain that he/she can ask you one question about the envelopes before deciding which envelope they want. Bring out the question: Which one has the blank paper? Give the volunteer the envelope of their choice.

Continue the assembly by pointing out to the pupils that throughout life they will have a number of important decisions to make; in these cases it is important to make the right decision. Illustrate the point by using the example of buying a car. Talk to the pupils about this being an informed choice; they need to know if the car is suitable for them, if it is good value. It's no use choosing a car just because you like the colour.

Go on to ask the pupils to give you more examples of decisions to be made; some important, some trivial. For each one, talk about the appropriate method of deciding. As you go through this process you might like to introduce some decision-making situations of your own, e.g. no money and hungry – should I steal those sweets?

Conclude the assembly by pointing out that, with some decisions, the main thing is that you are happy with your choice. Perhaps having decided to buy a particular type of car, you choose to buy a red one because you like the colour. With other decisions there is only one choice, because any other decision would be to do something wrong. Go back and illustrate this point with the moral decisions you have introduced, e.g. You cannot steal sweets because it is wrong.

**Related assemblies**  None

**Note**  With older pupils this assembly could be related to subject or career options.

# The love of money is the root of all evil

**Theme**   The unacceptability of greed

**Date**   No specific date

**Materials**   Ten large pieces of paper, each with one of the following words on: 'The love of money is the root of all evil'.
A table and chair for Midas to count money

**Assembly organization**   **B**efore the assembly choose four pupils to act out a mini-play. The parts are:

Midas             Midas's daughter
Dionysus         Midas's wife.

You will need to find time for the pupils to rehearse their actions before the assembly.

You will also need ten other pupils to hold up the words of the saying.

Start the assembly by asking the ten pupils to hold up the words of the saying in the correct order. Explain that the saying originally comes from the Bible and that you would like to try and illustrate what it might mean using an Ancient Greek myth about a king called Midas.

**Narrator**   Here we see Midas counting out his money. He is a kind and thoughtful king but he is very greedy.
○ *King Midas is seated at a table. He mimes counting his money. Enter Dionysus who walks over to Midas.*

**Narrator**   Dionysus is one of the many Greek gods who Midas has recently helped. Dionysus has come to repay Midas by granting him a wish.
○ *Midas looks thoughtful.*

**Narrator**   Midas decides to ask that everything he touches turn to gold.
○ *Dionysus agrees and then walks away.*

**Narrator**   Midas can't believe his luck – everything he touches is to turn to gold! So he tries out his wish by picking up an apple from a bowl of fruit on his desk.

O *Midas reaches across and mimes picking up an apple. He looks amazed.*

**Narrator**  Midas is amazed; he goes to find his family. The first person he finds is his daughter.

O *Midas gets up and excitedly walks over to his daughter. He takes hold of her arms and turns her to face him.*

**Narrator**  Can you predict what happens?
Yes! You are right! Midas's daughter turns to gold! Now the King is not so happy.

O *Midas returns to his seat and puts his head on the desk in despair. Midas's daughter remains absolutely still.*

**Narrator**  Now Midas's wife comes in to see what is upsetting him. She touches him on the shoulder to attract his attention, and is immediately turned to gold.

O *Midas's wife enters from behind. She walks over to Midas and touches his shoulder. Midas's wife now remains absolutely still.*

**Narrator**  Can you think what other problems Midas will have?

Bring out the answers: His food and drink will turn to gold.

**Narrator**  He has turned his whole family into gold and cannot eat or drink. What a very unhappy man he becomes.

O *Midas, wife and daughter remain in place while you explain the meaning of the story.*

Ask the pupils: What was it that made Midas unhappy? Help them to give the answer: It was his greed.
Now explain that this is not a true story, but that it helps to show how the love of money can be the cause of problems.
This is not to deny that money can be very useful. It is easier to use money than to exchange cows or potatoes or other things for what you need, as people used to do many years ago. The problems are caused by people loving money, by people being greedy. Finish the story by pointing out that Dionysus felt so sorry for Midas that he granted him another wish and took away

his gift. (You could also relate the story to the expression, 'having the Midas touch'.)

You could conclude the assembly by referring the pupils to the origins of this saying in the Bible. It also makes the point that we bring nothing into the world and can take nothing out. (See *1 Timothy 6, 6–10*)

**Related assemblies**   None

# Remembrance Sunday

This group of assemblies provides different ways of covering the topic of Remembrance Sunday. They can be used with different year groups.

An effective way of ending each of these assemblies is to ask the pupils to observe one minute's silence and then to leave the hall in silence.

**Assembly**
Why 11th November?

Walls have ears

The Battle of Britain

It's not a game

# Why 11th November?

**Theme**   Remembrance Sunday

**Date**   In the week before Remembrance Sunday

**Materials**   Poppy
Large map of Europe

**Assembly organization**   **S**tart by asking the pupils why you are wearing a poppy. Bring out the answer: In remembrance of the people who have died and been badly injured in wars. Explain that you want to look more closely at why people wear poppies and why they observe Remembrance Day.

Ask the pupils if anyone knows why 11 November is the important date. Explain that on the 11th hour of the 11th day in the 11th month in 1918, World War I came to an end.

On a large map of Europe show the pupils where World War I was fought: France, Belgium and North-eastern Italy. Explain that there was also fighting in Russia and Turkey but that British forces were mainly involved in the battles in France and Belgium. Ask if anyone knows the dates of World War I (1914–1918). Say that World War I was also called 'The Great War'.

Today's traditional poppy appeal and the British Legion were founded in 1921 by Earl Haig (the Commander-in-chief of the British forces in France and Belgium). The poppy was chosen for the appeal because poppies flowered around the graves of the dead. This was memorably recorded in John McCrae's poem entitled 'In Flanders Fields' (written during the Battle of Ypres, 1915).

Explain that the first Remembrance (or Armistice Day as it was called) was held in 1919 on 11 November to remember Britain's million dead from World War I. After World War II the date was changed to the second Sunday in November to remember those who died in both world wars.

Armistice Day was introduced because people were horrified by the large numbers who died in World War I. Explain that weapons of war were more advanced, enabling thousands of soldiers to be killed. During the first Battle of the Somme (one of the famous World War I battles), the British Army lost 60,000 soldiers on the first day. (Relate this figure to the population size of the nearest large town.) The battle lasted from 1 July to 18 November 1916, and by the end of the battle the Allied Army (British and French) had casualties of 800,000 soldiers.

Conclude by pointing out that it is important to remember those who died in the wars and that the money raised by selling poppies goes to help those who were injured and are still alive and needing support.

At this point you might wish to bring the pupils up to date and talk about some of the most recent wars British soldiers have fought in. Make it clear that soldiers are still being left injured from wars and are in need of support and help. You could cover the Falklands War which took place in 1982. A British force was sent into the South Atlantic to free the Falkland Islands which had been invaded and over-run by Argentinean forces.

You might also like to mention the Gulf War which took place in 1991 after Sadam Hussein and the Iraqi forces invaded and over-ran Kuwait. The United Nations sent a force including British soldiers to free Kuwait.

Finally, suggest that as the pupils now know a little more about the reasons behind Remembrance Sunday, they might like to buy a poppy for themselves. This will help them remember those who have died and help support those still alive.

**Related assemblies**

Walls have ears
The Battle of Britain
It's not a game

# Walls have ears

**Theme**  Remembrance Sunday

**Date**  In the week before Remembrance Sunday

**Materials**  Four large posters with the following war-time sayings:
Dig for victory
Be like dad. Keep mum.
Walls have ears.
Careless talk costs lives.
The following amounts of food:
2 oz (60 g) butter     2 oz (60 g) cheese
2 oz (60 g) bacon     1 lb (920 g) sugar
Poppy
Tape-recording of an air-raid siren (available on sound track records)

**Assembly organization**  Start by asking for four volunteers to hold up the posters.

Explain to the pupils that today you want to remember not only the hundreds of thousands of soldiers, sailors and airmen who died in World War II but also to look at how the war affected the civilian population. Thousands of ordinary people also died during the war.

Bring forward the volunteer with the 'Dig for Victory' poster. Ask the pupils if anyone can explain what this saying means? Bring out the answer: As food was in short supply, people were asked to dig up any spare ground and grow any food they could.

Go on to explain that food was in short supply because, from the very beginning of the war in 1939, German U-boats (submarines) in the Atlantic Ocean had been sinking merchant ships carrying food and other supplies. This became known as 'The Battle of the Atlantic' as the British tried to take convoys (large groups) of ships across the Atlantic protected by Royal Navy ships and German submarines tried to sink as many of the ships as they could. In the first three months of 1942, 1.6 million tons of Allied ships were sunk. By the end of the war approximately 12 million tons had been sunk and 27,000 British merchant seamen killed.

Ask the pupils if they can tell you how else the shortage of food affected people's lives. Bring out the answer: Food was rationed.

Show the pupils the examples of food rations and contrast them with how much we consume today:

- 2 oz butter, cheese and bacon per week
- 1 lb of sugar per month.

You could add that an adult also had only three pints of milk per week.

In addition to rationing, some foods were hardly seen by people in Britain. For example, most children grew up without ever seeing a banana. Fresh eggs were very difficult to come by so most people made do with powdered egg.

Point out that the ships that were sunk did not just carry food so many other things were in short supply. As a result clothing was also rationed, and metal fences and railings around parks were pulled up so the metal could be melted down to be used for making weapons (although little was actually used).

Next, tell the pupils that you want to play a sound that would have been very familiar to people during the war. Play the tape of the air-raid siren. Explain that this sound was used to warn the civilian population that an air raid was about to begin, that is that hundreds of enemy planes were about to fly overhead and drop thousands of bombs. British planes were sent out to try and stop them. Hundreds of pilots lost their lives defending Britain's cities.

The Battle of London began in late summer 1940. In this, London was bombed every night (as well as some day-time raids) from the end of August to the beginning of November. During this time many pilots and thousands of civilians lost their lives. This type of bombing raid was called 'The Blitz' coming from the German term *Blitzkrieg*, meaning lightning war. To reduce casualties during 'The Blitz' a number of things were done:

**Evacuation**    Young city children were moved out of their homes and away from their parents to live with families they did not know in the countryside.

**Blackout**   People put thick curtains up in their windows to stop light getting out. This was done because lights in the cities would give enemy planes targets to bomb. (In some cases fires were lit away from the cities to try and get enemy planes to drop their bombs in the wrong places.) People called ARP wardens patrolled the streets to make sure no lights were showing. (ARP = Air Raid Precaution)

**Air raid shelters**   In London people slept in bunk beds down in the Underground stations. In other cities people dug air-raid shelters (called Anderson shelters) in their back gardens and slept in them during night-time bombing raids.

**Barrage balloons**   An 'umbrella' of barrage balloons was flown over many cities. The wires they were attached to prevented low-level bombing attacks.

Conclude by looking at some of the other posters and explain their meanings:

- Be like dad. Keep mum.
- Walls have ears.
- Careless talk costs lives.

All these were to warn people of the danger of spies.

Finally, point out that when the pupils buy a poppy they should remember civilians who die in wars as well as those in the armed forces.

**Related assemblies**   Why 11th November?
The Battle of Britain
It's not a game

# The Battle of Britain

**Theme**  Remembrance Sunday

**Date**  In the week before Remembrance Sunday

**Materials**  Large map of Europe

**Assembly organization**  Start the assembly by saying that, fortunately, most of us today have never had to face the horrors of war. It is therefore very difficult for us to understand how frightening it must be to go into a battle knowing you could die or be seriously injured.

Explain to the pupils that Remembrance Sunday is concerned with remembering the people who were injured or killed in the battles of many wars – from World War I right up to the Gulf War in 1991. Tell them you would like to try to make them feel what it must have been like to be an eighteen- or nineteen-year-old ready to fight in one of the most famous battles of World War II.

To do this you will need to look at two of the famous events of the World War II:

The Dunkirk evacuation    26 May–3 June 1940
The Battle of Britain        July–October 1940

**The Dunkirk evacuation**  The British Expeditionary Force had been sent to stop the German Army advancing across Western Europe. It was forced back, however, and pinned down on the beaches around Dunkirk in northern France. (Indicate on a large map of Europe the directions the German troops had advanced across France. Show the final position of the British troops around Dunkirk.)

Between 26 May and midnight 3 June 1940 an armada of little ships picked up the soldiers of the British Expeditionary Force from the beaches around Dunkirk and carried them to England. From the original Force some 211,000 officers and men as well as 13,000 wounded and 110,000 French soldiers were rescued.

At this point you might like to read out the first-hand account of the Dunkirk evacuation given in the additional notes on page 110.

The Dunkirk evacuation was a great success but the soldiers had to wait a number of days on the beaches. During this time they were bombed and machine-gunned by enemy planes. When they left, much of their equipment was abandoned on the beaches. All this left the British Army in a very weak position to defend the country against an invasion by the German Army. The British Isles were almost defenceless and relied heavily on young RAF pilots to defend the skies.

During this early stage of the War, the British Army lost 4700 soldiers.

Next go on to read the following extract from Prime Minister Winston Churchill's speech. It was given on 18 June 1940 to the House of Commons, to help restore courage in a desperate situation.

> What General Weygand was called 'The Battle of France' is over, the Battle of Britain is about to begin; upon this Battle depends the survival of Christian Civilization, upon it depends our own British life and the long continuity of our institutions and our Empire. The whole fury and might of the enemy must very soon be turned on us. Hitler knows he will have to break us in this island or lose the war.

**The Battle of Britain**

In June 1940 only Great Britain stood between Hitler and his conquest of the whole of Western Europe. On aerodromes from Norway to France, the German Luftwaffe (airforce) made preparations for the invasion of Britain. They were to carry out air-raids intended to prepare the way for the invasion troops.

The Germans had 5000 aircraft while the Royal Air Force had only 750 fighters (28 squadrons of Hurricanes, 20 of Spitfires, 8 of Blenheims and 2 of Defiants). Of these only the Spitfires and Hurricanes would be of any use. This made the German superiority approximately 10 to 1.

Remind the pupils to consider how, as young pilots, they would have felt facing such numerically superior odds. They would also have known how important it was to the country's defence that they should win the forthcoming battle.

Conclude this section of the assembly with some statistics from the battle:

- Some 1700 German aircraft were destroyed (many of

their crews would have been killed) and 643 were damaged.

- The RAF lost 915* aircraft, and 1495 pilots and other personnel were killed.

*This number is greater than the number of aeroplanes at the start of the battle as new ones were built during the battle.

At this point you might like to read out the account given by a Spitfire pilot, in the additional notes on page 111.

The Battle of Britain was such an important battle, and fought by so few pilots, that Prime Minister Churchill said at its end: 'Never in the field of human conflict was so much owed by so many to so few.'

Finally, remind the pupils of how frightening war must be. When they buy their poppies they do so not only to remember the young men and women who died in World War II but also to remember those who have died in the many wars since then, right up to the 1991 Gulf War. Make it clear that the money goes to help the thousands of men and women who have been injured in these wars.

**Related assemblies**

Why 11th November?
Walls have ears
It's not a game

**Additional notes**

**The Dunkirk evacuation**

This is a first-hand account from a Gunnery officer. (For younger pupils you might like to edit out parts of this account.)

There were lines of men waiting in queues until boats arrived to transport them, 20 or so a time, to the steamers and warships. The queue stood there fixed and regular, no bunching, no pushing.

Stepping over the bodies we marched on to the beach. A horrible stench of blood and mutilated flesh pervaded the place. There was no escape from it. We might have been walking through a slaughterhouse on a hot day.

**The Battle of Britain**

This is a Spitfire pilot's account of his experiences.

The bullets from your eight guns go pumping into his belly. He begins to smoke. But the wicked tracer sparkles and flashes over the top of your cockpit and you break into a tight turn. Now you have two enemies. The Messerschmitt 109 on your tail and your remorseless ever-present opponent – the force of gravity. Over your shoulder you can still see the ugly, questing snout of the 109. You tighten the turn. The Spitfire protests and shudders and when the blood drains from your eyes you 'grey out'. But you keep turning. For life itself is at stake.

# It's not a game

**Theme** Remembrance Sunday

**Date** In the week before Remembrance Sunday

**Materials** None

**Assembly organization** Ask the pupils how many of them have computer games they play at home. Go on to talk about the number of such games which involve fighting and killing, and how they make it fun. Relate this point to the films which make out war to be a game, where heroes kill the evil enemy.

Explain to the pupils that today you would like to look at what it is really like to go to war, through the eyes of some of the soldiers who fought in World War I.

The following section of the assembly is made up of extracts from poems, each of which covers an aspect of war. Each extract you use should be read to the pupils by yourself or a member of your form, and followed by a few comments from yourself to help bring out the meaning behind the words.

*Before the battle* **Exposure** by Wilfred Owen

Our brains ache, in the merciless iced east winds that knife us...
Wearied we keep awake because the night is silent...
Low, dropping flares confuse our memory of the salient...
Worried by silence, sentries whisper, curious, nervous,
  But nothing happens.

Watching, we hear the mad gusts tugging on the wire,
Like twitching agonies of men among its brambles.
Northward, incessantly, the flickering gunnery rumbles,
Far off, like a dull rumour of some other war.
  What are we doing here?

**During the battle**   **Bombardment**  by Richard Aldington

Four days the earth was rent and torn
By bursting steel,
The houses fell about us;
Three nights we dared not sleep,
Sweating and listening for the imminent crash
Which meant our death.

The fourth night every man,
Nerve-tortured, racked to exhaustion,
Slept, muttering and twitching,
While the shells crashed overhead.

**The enemy**   **The man he killed**  by Thomas Hardy

'Had he and I but met
By some old ancient inn,
We should have sat us down to drink.

'But ranged as infantry,
And staring face to face,
I shot at him as he at me,
And killed him in his place.

'I shot him dead because –
Because he was my foe.
Just so my foe of course he was;
That's clear enough...'
(Adapted to make it more meaningful to children)

To further emphasize the futile nature of one man
shooting another because they are enemies, you could
mention that during World War I, on Christmas Day, the
soldiers of all sides would stop fighting, and play games
together. The next day, however, they would go back to
killing each other.

*In memory of the dead*

### After Blenheim  by Robert Southey

They say it was a shocking sight
After the field was won;
For many thousand bodies here
Lay rotting in the sun.
But things like that, you know, must be
After a famous victory.

### In Flanders field  by John McCrae

In Flanders fields the poppies blow
Between the crosses, row on row,
That mark our place, and in the sky
The larks, still bravely singing, fly
Scarce heard amid the guns below.

We are the Dead. Short days ago
We lived, felt dawn, saw sunset glow,
Loved and were loved, and now we lie
In Flanders fields.

### Six young men  by Ted Hughes

This one was shot in an attack and lay
Calling in the wire, then this one, his best friend,
Went out to bring him in and was shot too;
And this one, the very moment he was warned
From potting at tin cans in no-man's land,
Fell back dead with his rifle-sights shot away.
The rest, nobody knows what they came to,
But come to the worst they must have done, and held it
Closer than their hope; all were killed.

### The last post  by Robert Graves

The bugler sent a call of high romance –
'Lights out! Lights out!' to the deserted square:
On the thin brazen notes he threw a prayer,
'God, if it's *this* for me next time in France...
O spare the phantom bugle as I lie
Dead in the gas and smoke and roar of guns,
Dead in a row with the other broken ones,
Lying so stiff and still under the sky,
Jolly young Fusiliers, too good to die.'
The music ceased, and the red sunset flare
Was blood about his head as he stood there.

*The survivors*

### Disabled by Wilfred Owen

He sat in a wheeled chair, waiting for dark,
And shivered in his ghastly suit of grey,
Legless, sewn short at elbow. Through the park
Voices of boys rang saddening like a hymn,
Voices of play and pleasure after day,
Till gathering sleep had mothered them from him.

### A lament by Wilfred Wilson Gibson

We who are left, how shall we look again
Happily on the sun, or feel the rain,
Without remembering how they who went
Ungrudgingly, and spent
Their all for us, loved, too, the sun and rain?

After reading a selection of these poems, go on to talk to the pupils about how it is clear from these words of men who lived through war that it is not like they see it in films or video games. War is a terrible experience which, even if you survive, affects you for the rest of your life.

Remind the pupils that, as Remembrance Sunday approaches, they can buy a poppy to help those who survived the wars and are injured or disabled. In wearing their poppies they should remember the thoughts of those who lived through war.

Conclude the assembly by reading one of the following poem extracts to the pupils.

### The soldier by Rupert Brooke

If I should die, think only this of me:
That there's some corner of a foreign field
That is for ever England.

### For the fallen (September 1914) by Laurence Binyon

They shall grow not old, as we that are left grow old,
Age shall not weary them, nor the years condemn.
At the going down of the sun and in the morning,
We will remember them.

**Related assemblies**

Why 11th November?
Walls have ears
The Battle of Britain

# Saints' Days

In this section I have included four assemblies covering the patron saints of the British Isles. Whichever of these assemblies you use first, you might like to start by explaining the meaning of patron saint. A suitable explanation might be: Someone who has been officially recognized by the Church as being a very holy person who has gained recognition and a high place in heaven. This person has then been chosen by a country or group of people as an individual to be held up as a good example for people to follow.

| Assembly | Saint's day |
|---|---|
| St Valentine | 14 February |
| St David | 1 March |
| St Patrick | 17 March |
| St George | 23 April |
| St Andrew | 30 November |
| St Nicholas | 6 December |

# St Valentine

**Theme** St Valentine's Day

**Date** In the week of 14 February

**Materials** Box
Five small pieces of paper
Five pens
Bay leaf

**Assembly organization** **S**tart the assembly by asking the pupils if they can tell you on which day that week is St Valentine's Day. Go on to say that it's at this time of year when living things come out of winter and start to show signs of life. People used to believe that birds started to mate and build their nests on St Valentine's Day. Some even believed this happened because St Valentine had spoken to the birds.

Next move on to explain who St Valentine was. Point out that there are many people who are linked to the origins of St Valentine and Valentine's Day traditions. One legend says that St Valentine was put into prison in AD 270 because of his Christian beliefs. (You might like to explain that at this time the Romans ruled most of the known world. They believed in many different gods and punished Christians for their belief in one god.) While in prison St Valentine cured the blindness of his jailer's daughter, for which miracle he was sentenced to death. (You might like to suggest that this miracle was seen as an example of his Christian beliefs, which was why he was sentenced to death.)

The night before he was due to be executed St Valentine wrote a note to the jailer's daughter, whom he had fallen in love with, which he is believed to have signed 'Your Valentine'. On 14 February St Valentine was executed. After his death, St Valentine was said to keep watch over all those who were in true love.

Go on to say that some of the customs that have existed may be due to this story. Two of which you might like to mention are:

- The belief that the first male a girl sees (outside her own family) on 14 February is the person she will marry. (Perhaps the girls had better keep their eyes closed!)

● The belief that on 13 February a girl dreams of the boy she will marry. To influence their dreams some girls would pin a bay leaf (hold up your bay leaf) to their pillow. Others would eat a boiled egg, shell as well, having first replaced the yolk with salt. (Make it clear that this should not be tried!)

Next ask for five boys and five girls to volunteer to help you in another tradition dating back to the Middle Ages. Give each boy a piece of paper and a pen, then ask them to write their name on the paper. Tell them to fold it and put it into the box. Now ask the girls to pick out one piece of paper and then to stand with the boy whose name is on it.

Explain that this custom is mentioned as far back as the fourteenth century. Those chosen in this way would be accepted as sweethearts or valentines for the next year and the couples would exchange gifts.

At some point cards began to replace these gifts and this may explain the Valentine's Day tradition of sending cards. The exact origin, however, is not clear. Valentine cards went out of fashion until 1926 when the custom was revived.

Allow the volunteers to return to their places and suggest that perhaps they are glad we have abandoned the tradition of picking out names at random. Sending anonymous Valentine's cards is much safer.

Conclude the assembly by reminding the pupils on which day of the week Valentine's Day falls.

**Related assemblies**   None

# St David

**Theme**   St David's Day

**Date**   In the week of 1 March

**Materials**   Welsh flag
Leek
Daffodil
Small sign with the date 1 March clearly written on it

**Assembly organization**   **A**sk for four volunteers to come out to the front of the assembly and hold up the items listed above. Ask the rest of the pupils if they can tell you what the connection is between the items at the front of the assembly. Bring out the answer: Wales. Explain to the pupils the connection between each item and Wales.

**Welsh flag**   The country of Wales is part of the British Isles but it has this flag as its own.

**Daffodils and leeks**   These two items have become emblems associated with Wales. They are worn by Welsh people on their national day. The origin of these emblems is not known but several stories suggest an explanation. One story says that during the seventh century AD Welsh soldiers fighting the Saxons wore a leek to distinguish themselves. It is thought that the connection with the daffodil comes from the Welsh name for David – *Dafydd* – which sounds similar. You could also suggest a possible connection between daffodils and 1 March when they will usually be in flower.

**1 March**   This is St David's Day. St David is the patron saint of Wales. Give pupils the following information about St David.

- He was the only British saint who actually lived and worked in his own country.

- He spent his life in Wales building monasteries (about twelve), including Glastonbury and Menevia (later renamed St David's).

- St David is believed to have lived in the seventh century, dying in AD 660.

- His father was Sant, a chief of Cardigan, and his mother St Non.

- He is believed to have been educated by a scribe called Paulinus and later to have restored Paulinus's sight. (You may like to explain the word 'scribe' as a person who copied out religious books. There were no printing presses in those days.)

St David and the monks, who lived in the monasteries he built, led an austere life.

- They did not use cattle to plough their fields.
- They spent a great deal of time studying in silence.
- They lived mainly on vegetables, bread and water.

St David is also known as 'the waterman', possibly for two reasons:

- his refusal to drink alcohol, instead living by drinking water, or

- his habit of plunging himself into cold water as an act of austerity. (You might like to explain this as meaning a way of making his life harsher.)

Conclude the assembly by reminding the pupils which day in the week is St David's Day.

| | |
|---|---|
| **Related assemblies** | St Andrew |
| | St George |
| | St Patrick |

# St Patrick

**Theme**   St Patrick's Day

**Date**   In the week of 17 March

**Materials**   Union flag (a large paper replica will do)
Twelve sheets of paper with the following information written on one sheet each:

| | | |
|---|---|---|
| St David | 1 March | Wales |
| St Patrick | 17 March | Ireland |
| St George | 23 April | England |
| St Andrew | 30 November | Scotland |

**Assembly organization**   Ask for twelve volunteers and give each a sheet of paper. Tell them not to show the information to the rest of the pupils.

Start the assembly by asking the four pupils with the patron saints' names to show their information. Ask the rest of the pupils if they can tell you the connection between the four names. Bring out the answer: They are the patron saints of England, Scotland, Ireland and Wales.

Next ask the pupils holding the four countries' names to show their information. Ask the rest of the pupils to match the country to its patron saint.

Finally ask the pupils holding the four dates of the saints days to show their information. Ask the rest of the pupils to match the dates to the patron saints. Tell the assembly that today you want to talk about Saint Patrick.

Collect in the information regarding the other three patron saints, then remind the pupils of the information regarding St Patrick. (Keep the St Patrick information on display throughout the assembly.)

Go on to talk about St Patrick's life. You might like to recount the following episodes:

● As a child he was taken by force from his home in either England or France (it is not clear where he was born) and transported to Ireland. Here he was sold to a chief called Milchu.

● While he looked after Milchu's animals in the fields, St Patrick felt sad and lonely because he missed his family and friends. Then he remembered that he could talk to God in his prayers. After that he prayed in the mornings when he woke up, during the day and at the end of the day before he went to sleep. One day a voice spoke to him and told him to return home. It is not clear if he escaped or was released.

- After his return home St Patrick went to study in the monastery at Tours in France. He was later made Bishop of Ireland by Pope Celestine I and returned to Ireland as a missionary, travelling all over the country preaching, and building churches and monasteries. He converted many of the Irish chiefs to Christianity, including Milchu.

- Two legends connected with Patrick are:

  1 he related Christian belief in the Holy Trinity (God, Jesus and the Holy Spirit) to the three leaves of the shamrock plant
  2 he freed Ireland from snakes.

You could conclude the assembly by showing pupils the union flag and pointing out it contains the:
red diagonal cross of St Patrick
red cross of St George
white diagonal cross on a blue background of St Andrew.
The cross of St Patrick was added to the flag in the early 1800s.

**Related assemblies**   St George
St David
St Andrew

# St George

**Theme**    The legend of St George

**Date**    In the week of 23 April

**Materials**    Copies of the Union flag and St George's flag (These can be drawn on large sheets of paper and coloured in)

**Assembly organization**    **B**efore the assembly choose eleven pupils from your form to act out a short play. They will need time to practise their roles:

St George    Three townspeople
Princess    Five daughters
Dragon

At the beginning of the assembly, ask the actors to get into position and explain to the remaining pupils that you want them to watch a short play. At the end you would like them to tell you who the story is about.

**Narrator**    Here we see the people of a town called Silene bringing out a sheep and tying it up outside the town.
    ○ *Townspeople mime pulling out a sheep and tie it to a chair. Then go back into the town.*

**Narrator**    Having tied up the sheep, the townspeople return home before the dragon comes out to eat it.
    ○ *Dragon comes over and mimes eating the sheep.*

**Narrator**    Eventually the dragon ate all the townspeople's sheep and they had no more to feed to the dragon. The townspeople were now very worried as the dragon said that unless he was fed he would come out and eat some of them.
    When all the sheep had gone the people fed their daughters to the dragon. The girls had to draw lots to decide who should be tied up outside the town.
    ○ *Princess and other daughters mime drawing lots. Princess looks frightened.*

**Narrator**    Today the Princess is to be given to the dragon. Here we see the townspeople taking her out of the town and tying her up.

○ *Townspeople come over and take the Princess away. They mime tying her to a chair.*

**Narrator**  Now the dragon appears and comes over to eat the Princess. A knight passes by. He offers to kill the dragon and free the Princess if the people will be baptized and become Christians.

○ *Knight walks over from the opposite side and talks to the townspeople. He then walks over to the dragon and mimes killing it with his sword. Next he turns and mimes releasing the Princess.*

Ask the pupils what was the name of the knight. Bring out the answer: St George.

Point out to the pupils that there are many legends about St George but that he became famous in England after the Crusades, when he became patron sain of soldiers. Legend had it that he appeared as a heavenly figure at a number of battles (including the battle of Antioch), helping the Crusaders to defeat the Saracens.

St George finally became patron saint of England following the battle of Agincourt in 1415. It was claimed that many soldiers saw him riding in the sky above the battle.

Ask the pupils which day is St George's Day. Bring out the answer: 23 April. Ask two pupils to come out to hold up the Union flag and St George's flag. Ask the pupils to name the two flags.

Next ask the pupils to look at the two flags and explain any connection they can see between them. Bring out the answer: The Union flag contains the red cross of the flag of St George.

Conclude the assembly by reminding the pupils which day is St George's Day in that week.

**Related assemblies**  St Andrew
St David
St Patrick

# St Andrew

**Theme**     St Andrew's Day

**Date**     In the week of 30 November

**Materials**     Copies of the Union flag and St Andrew's flag (These can be drawn on large sheets of paper and coloured in)

**Assembly organisation**     **A**sk two pupils to come out to hold up the Union flag and St Andrew's flag.

Start the assembly by asking the pupils if they can tell you the names of the two flags. Next ask which country St Andrew's flag represents. Bring out the answer: Scotland. Go on to ask the pupils if they can tell you why the Scots use the flag of St Andrew. Bring out the answer: St Andrew is the patron saint of Scotland. Next ask the pupils if they can tell you which day is St Andrew's Day. Bring out the answer: 30 November.

Go back to look at the two flags with the pupils and ask if they can see a connection between them. Bring out the answer: The Union flag contains the cross of St Andrew's flag. You might like to point out that the Union flag also contains the red cross of St George and the diagonal red cross of St Patrick. If you wish you can add that the white cross of St Andrew was added to the red cross of St George when James VI of Scotland became King James I of England.

Next, ask the pupils if they can tell you who St Andrew was. What was it that made him famous? Bring out the answer: He was one of the disciples (followers) of Jesus. Follow this by asking the pupils how many disciples there were and what their names were?

| Peter | Andrew | Judas Iscariot |
| Thomas | Matthew | Judas |
| James | Philip | John |
| Simon | James | Bartholomew |

Go on to explain that Andrew was a fisherman with his brother Peter. They both became disciples when Jesus saw them fishing on Lake Galilee and said to them: 'Come with me and I will make you fishers of men'. (See *Matthew 4, 18–22*)

If you wish you could also talk to the pupils

about the story of the five loaves and two fishes, pointin
out that it was Andrew who first noticed the boy with th
loaves and fishes. (See *John 6, 1–15*)

Like many of the early followers of Jesus,
Andrew was killed for his beliefs. He was crucified at
Patras in Greece on an X-shaped cross. This is
remembered in the shape of the white cross on the flag o
St Andrew.

Pupils may think it strange that a man who
lived and died thousands of miles away from Scotland
became Scotland's patron saint. Explain that it is because
his bones are believed to have been brought from Patras,
where he was crucified, to what is now St Andrews in
Scotland.

Mention that St Andrew is also the patron sain
of Russia and of fishermen. In this country we regard hir
mainly as the patron saint of Scotland.

Conclude the assembly by reminding the
pupils which day that week is St Andrew's Day.

**Related**
**assemblies**

St George
St David
St Patrick

# St Nicholas

**Theme**  St Nicholas's day

**Date**  Beginning of December

**Materials**  None

**Assembly organization**

**A**sk the pupils how many of them have got advent calendars. How many of them have got the ones with small chocolates inside? Say that advent calendars are a count-down to Christmas when they will, of course, get presents from Father Christmas. (With older pupils reference to 'Father Christmas' will introduce an element of humour into the assembly.) Point out that in some countries in Europe children do not have to wait so long to get their presents.

Ask the pupils if they know who it is who brings children small presents in places like Germany, before Christmas. Bring out the answer: St Nicholas. Ask on what day does St Nicholas bring round his presents. Bring out the answer: The night of 5 December (eve of St Nicholas's Day – 6 December).

You might like to add that this is believed to be the eve of the date of his death (6 December).

Explain that exactly what St Nicholas did, and who he was, is not clear, except that he probably lived in a place called Lycia (a province of Asia in the Roman Empire). and that he became Archbishop of Lycia. He finally died somewhere around AD 400.

Nicholas is thought to have brought three children back to life. They had been murdered and had their bodies placed in a tub of salty water. Because of this St Nicholas is the patron saint of children.

One explanation for gifts being given to children on the night of 5 December may be that St Nicholas was believed to have secretly left gifts of gold bars at the house of a poor family, so the father could give them as dowry gifts at each of his three daughters' weddings. (You might want to explain the tradition of dowry gifts.) So that is why in some countries on 5 December, children leave out hay, straw or carrots for

St Nicholas's horse. They also leave out a shoe which
St Nicholas fills with sweets or leaves a small present.

In Holland people give presents on
5 December. They are meant to be a surprise so
sometimes they are hidden or small presents are
concealed in large boxes.

The legend of St Nicholas was taken to America
by Dutch settlers. In America his name became shortened
to Sinta Class which, in English, soon became Santa
Claus. In England during the sixteenth century,
St Nicholas was replaced by the cheerful character of
Father Christmas. Eventually Santa Claus and Father
Christmas became seen as the same person, but no one is
clear how St Nicholas's horse became Santa Claus's
reindeer.

Conclude the assembly by reminding pupils
which day is St Nicholas's Day.

**Related
assemblies**   None